At The Hands Of Him

Everything happen...
A.T.H.O.H.

P.S. Tell a friend too!

At The Hands Of Him

My Journey Of Betrayal To Hidden Blessings

Rhlonda Washington

At The Hands of H(h)im

The Cataloging-in – Publication data is on file with the Library of Congress. Library of Congress Control Number: 2021905053

Printed in the United States of America

2021-First edition

Book design by Lucy Holtsnider

ISBN: 978-1-7365281-0-5

FREE GUIDE!

My Daily Declaration

Download this free guide at AtTheHandsOfHim.com. Inside you will find a declaration to start your day and a playlist to listen to during your time of devotion.

God made my life complete when I placed
all the pieces before him.

When I got my act together, he gave me a fresh start.
Now I'm alert to God 's ways; I don't take God for granted.
Every day I review the ways he works; I try not to miss a trick.
I feel put back together, and I'm watching my step.
God rewrote the text of my life when I opened the book of my heart to his eyes.

Psalms 18:20-24 (MSG)

Dedication

My Parents-Sonja and George~

Honor your father and your mother, so that you may live long in the land the Lord your God is giving you. Exodus 20:12

I am blessed to have a mom and dad like you two.
Thank you for raising me to have a relationship with Jesus and to trust that God's hand can and will hold me always.
Mom, you are my rock and Dad you are my boulder.

My Sons~ Jewel & Terrance

Come my children, listen to me; I will teach you the fear of the Lord. Psalms 34:11

Thank you for understanding my pain and never holding it against me. Thank you for just being there

My girls~

Lovers of God give good advice to their friends. Proverbs 12:26(TPT)

Bev~ My BFF always. Thanks for holding the mirror for me. Every phone call and even some kicks in the butt, you reminded me of the gift I have to share. What a precious gift you are to me.
Shamera~ who would have thought that this book would be the thing to bring us together as friends.
Thank you, friend! "Go to work God! Go to work!"
Tammy Ms. 3.0~ your words of inspiration and confirmationhelped me on more days that you can imagine. Thank you for always having a Godly perspective that helped me with this project.

To friends old and new~

Sweet friendships refresh the soul and awaken our hearts with joy. Proverbs 27:9 (TPT)

Be encouraged and hold your head up high!
You're not alone. You are no longer betrayed.
I say you are blessed...and so does God!

To the one who betrayed me ~

You intended to harm me, but God intended it for good to accomplish what is now being done, the saving of many lives. Genesis 50:20
Thank You.

Contents

Preface

"All praise to the God and Father of our Master, Jesus the Messiah! Father of all mercy! God of all healing counsel! He comes alongside us when we go through hard times, and before you know it, he brings us alongside someone else who is going through hard times so that we can be there for that person just as God was there for us." 2 Corinthians 1:3-4 (MSG)

Are you hurting from a breakup now that the relationship is over? Do you feel hoodwinked or conned? How about betrayed? Not just any ol' betrayal; I mean the worst kind of betrayal. Are you ready to dig deep into understanding why you, of all people, had to experience this horrible offense? I get it, maybe not. However, if you've experienced betrayal at the hands of someone you loved deeply, and, more than blindsided you, it left you feeling completely hopeless, I want you to come along with me for a moment.

My friend—yes, you are my friend because we're in this together—before you read my story, I must be sincerely honest; this is one of the hardest things I've ever decided to do. I wrestled with being vulnerable and gutting myself open for all to see. I also considered the judgment and possible backlash or criticism that could come from sharing my story. You see, I'm pulling back all the layers, opening up my soul, and sharing a very dark place in my life with the world. It's not anything to brag about, nor was it pretty.

I'm sure you're wondering, "Why tell it then?" Well, I have to tell it because I made it through the betrayal, which was complete healing for me, and I believe it can be for you too. I also know there is a woman (perhaps even a man) who's gone through something very similar and may still be "dealing" with the aftershocks. Or, maybe a woman smack dab in the middle of it right now, feeling alone, hurt, lost, confused, and, yes, betrayed. I believe there could be a young lady who will come across this book, and it will help her recognize the "red flags" and stand firm and say, "No...Not me. Not today. Not ever!"

I won't put on airs and say I wasn't afraid to tell my story. I was so afraid that I put it off for over two years. I was paralyzed by fear and what people would have to say about me putting it all out there. Trust me; I thought of everything. I thought people would think I was bitter; I was attacking my ex-husband; I was playing the victim; I was selfish and doggish; my ex played me like a fool or I was flat out stupid. And you know what? At some point or another, I'll admit I was all of those things. But one thing I know for sure about sharing my story is that I couldn't "wish" it away as much as I tried. *Growing,* not going, through the healing, I heard "at the hands of Him" or saw the words in something I read. I mean, it was everywhere. It finally dawned on me that I wasn't going to get to where His hands (God's) were leading me until I surrendered the fear over to Him and tell the truth about betrayal and blessings. I just couldn't let those erroneous thoughts stop me from putting it out there if it meant someone else could start to heal from their pain, especially if they knew they weren't alone.

I believe that women, in particular, will share some of their heartaches and heartbreaks with other female friends but still carry the pretense of "Honey, I'm all right, I'm fine." When the truth is, they're breaking or already broken inside. We try desperately to cover it up. We pull our shoulders back and put on a good face to save face. I'm not judging. I'm just saying we have a hard time being real about it. Trust me. I get it; I do. It's hard to muster up the courage and admit, "Girl, this thing is about to take me outta here. I'm beyond broken, I'm shattered. And I'm shattered into a thousand pieces and don't see a way out of this." We tell ourselves privately and others in confidence, "I feel like a fool 'cause I thought I was better than that. I would never let anyone do something like this to me, especially a man." Right? Is that not what we say, ladies? BUT wait a minute... you did. And guess what? I did too.

So, let me be clear. This book is raw, and it's real. Every experience, emotion, and thought I had was real. I don't mind gutting myself open to sharing the hurt, betrayal, and disappointment. It made me look at the truth, learn why it happened, and move toward the "now what?" That's why we're here, together. I'm hopeful that sharing my story is going to help free someone else.

It's also imperative that you understand that this isn't just about "him" the betrayer but also about "*HIM*" the blesser. Along this journey, I had to deal with much hurt at the hands of my ex-husband, but through it all God's hand, held and healed me. Even though *his* hand betrayed me, *HIS* hand moved me from betrayal to blessings throughout the entire process. Oh, don't think you're going to read through this book without me showing you God's hand without going to the Bible for strength, truth, encouragement, and His promises. My friend, rest assure that God's promises are always yes and amen. You'll see; keep reading.

Now, since I'm writing this book in the most authentic part

of who I am, there will be some "real talk," slang, or whatever you wanna call it. Don't go judging me if I give it to you the way it was at that moment, talking about..."Uhm did she use that cuss word? She said she loves God." I DO. But I refuse to be fake, and not only that but I'm still a work in progress. So, could you do me a favor? Chill, curl up in a comfy chair, bed, or whatever, and go along with me on this journey of betrayal to blessings.

Introduction

When you reach what some may call the "seasoned age" in life, there are some things you no longer entertain. You understand that your time is valuable, and you don't have time to play games with people. May I suggest the games of manipulation, deceit, and all the rest of the ugly games people play? It's true. Most people are past all the senseless gossiping to stay up on what's going on in the "shade room." But most of all, we no longer want to play with love or other people's hearts. Now, why do you suppose that is? For me, the answer is quite simple; because you're ready. You're ready to develop meaningful friendships, ready to treat people fairly, give them a chance, or at least the benefit of the doubt. You've accepted that you're not all that yourself, so you open your heart and mind to understand other people's struggles or shortcomings and not hold it against them.

Hopefully, we've matured to do so without judgment. But... but...but, hang on now. In all sincerity and, most of all, we're ready to settle down. Right? Settle down in every area of our lives. We're ready to settle down in our finances and get our money right, settle down on the time and energy we put into things that really don't serve us, and settle down and let go of the mess that will never add value to us. Even more so, we settle into our spiritual being's awareness to find peace within and with our purpose. Does this sound familiar?

Well, what about settling down with love? I'm talking about the kind of love you have with that one person to share lifelong experiences, memories, and eventually grow old together. If we're honest, no one wants to go through life without having someone to share their love with. I know we have family, friends, and, yes, we need our coworkers for an occasional happy hour outing. But don't we want that one person and everything else that we can call our own. We arrive at these places in life, especially where love is concerned because we've been there and done that, and it's gotten us nowhere but alone. Ahhhh, love. Yep. We're ready for THAT kind of love.

Well, what happens when you think you've found that person, only to find out later they weren't the "one" they told you they were and betrayed all of what you found yourself ready to pursue? You feel me already, huh? Yep, I knew it. I'm sure that what I'm about to share with you may feel like you're looking in a mirror. Right now, if you're honest, you're either going through something or have gone through a level of betrayal at the hands of someone you loved, and, quite frankly, it's hard to breathe. Not believe.... breathe! I mean, that joker knocked the breath out of you, and you didn't know how you were going to catch a gasp of air that would save you from dying. I know. I know. I can see you shaking your head right now with tears in the corner of your eyes. You know what? Please do me a favor. Go ahead and cry. I mean, get ugly with it. As a matter of fact, put this book down and dig deep into your soul. Do that kind of crying that will only get God's attention. Trust that your tears are liquid words to Him. You know what? I'll do it with you. C'mon, let it go. Cry, my friend. Let those tears of betrayal become the nutrients needed to water your blessing. That's right, get it all out.

All right, all right. There now. You feel a little better now? I do too. But you know what? You're getting through this. I know you will because you can't stay stuck! We've all been stuck at some point in our love relationships before, if not right now.

And it's all because of what somebody else did. Uh Hahn, not so fast. Think about it before you go into..."you damn right, it was them... Who do they think...I did so and so....and they did...." Yeah, I get it. I get all of that, and I feel you. However, when it's all said and done, what happened wasn't entirely "them" the way you think. It's just what happened and what you didn't expect to happen to you.

Look, I shall not tell a lie. Before getting into a relationship with my ex, I had everything I could imagine. I'll go ahead and say it. I was somewhat of a boss chick. I didn't need anybody to tell me that I had it going on because I knew it. My life was better than good. If I may (and I can), let me brag a little bit here. Lean in and check this out for a minute. I consider myself to be attractive. I had the bomb job in HR (check). I was making that money, honey (check).

I had a BS and Master's degree (check). Uh-huh, c'mon now. A single mom raised two sons without incident of the stereotypical kind, like a juvenile delinquent, jail, or teenage father. I put them both through college earning degrees, and both are doing very well for themselves, I might add (check). My credit score was high 700s (check). I had no debt (besides student loans, urgh) (check). I had money in the bank (check). Bills were paid on time and sometimes before the due date (check). I lived in an upscale area in North Dallas (check). My prayer life was on point, and my relationship with God was kicking (check). I mean, damn, what more could a chick ask for or worry about in life? What do people say nowadays? I was "living my best life." I know some of ya'll reading this are saying, "Sis, me too...yep, that was me too, so don't judge me.

I knew who I was back then (well, I thought I knew), and I wasn't ashamed, good, bad, and in progress. I didn't take any mess, but I had a big ol' heart. I was a straight shooter, no chaser. Okay, I had mouth sometimes (well, most of the time), but at least I meant what I said. All I'm trying to say is I was right, and I was all right with me. Oh, let me add this sidebar. I did the work from past relationships to learn the lessons needed for future ones. I certainly didn't want to make the same mistakes from previous relationships.

I took inventory to determine what worked for me and what didn't. Most of all, I had to ensure I had control over my relationships. The one thing I made a point to do was to take a step back to reevaluate my life and the choices I'd made. I finally enjoyed where I was in life, and the person I'd had grown to become. Look, I'm a planner. I like things to be a certain way, and when they're not, I tend to get a little bit edgy, but it's all good. At least I know that about me and can own my truth about it. When it comes to matters of the heart, I want my relationships to be a certain way. After all, I've seen all the bullshit before. I can admit that I love hard, and I love long because I tend to be a very loyal person and trust people right from the jump. I'd do anything for the people I love, even if that meant sacrificing what I wanted to make sure they had what they needed.

Getting back to the point, before I tell you about "his and HIS" hand, I had it all together. My heart was open to finding the right one, my intentions were coming from a good place, and it was time for me to get out and date again. But, this time, it was going to be different because I was different. This time, yo girl had a plan. I was going to use one of these dating apps, which I'd never done before, to see who was out there. I was in a new city, and I needed to seek out new adventures. Well, this time, I was going to be very selective in my choice, vet him thoroughly by talking over the phone for a few months (ask lots and lots of questions) before he laid eyes on me. I'd get to know him, and he'd get to know me. BAM! Now that's a plan!

I was careful. I was intentional. I set boundaries. But most of all, I was in control. Or, so I thought.

After mapping out the plan precisely, I pulled out my laptop, got comfortable on my chaise lounge with a glass of wine in hand. Before, I'd done a little research on online dating and asked a couple of people I knew who tried it for themselves. I created a profile and selected the pics to go along with it. After that, I got real cozy, took a sip.... logged into Black People Meet dot (damn) com, and something happened.

But first, let's start at the beginning.

At the Hands of him

CHAPTER ONE

Introducing "him"

"Can somebody, anybody, tell me what the hell just happened? There is no way this could be happening right now. No way, not now. How could he do this to me? After all the shit I went through trying to be a good wife to him, he decides to walk the hell out. What about all the sacrifices I made for him, living a life of being invisible to my own damn husband. You mean to tell me he get to walk out and leave his post? Leave me? With the bills, the house, and no income coming in right now? He must have lost his damn mind. Who the hell does he think I am? Without me, he couldn't have done half the shit he was able to do or get. Don't he know it was because of me that he could live comfortably in a nice clean home with a hot meal every day? And he has the audacity to freaking walk out without so much as an explanation? Okay. Okay". Breathe Rho, just breathe."

That was me. Those were the thoughts that raced through my mind that tragic day, September 16, 2018. The day I will never forget. The day my life would no longer be the same. It would no longer be the same because he threw down his hands, my life, our marriage, and everything else away the moment he decided to walk away. It was just a simple argument (again). An argument that I'd gotten accustomed to having that it didn't seem much out of the ordinary. But no, this time, the argument was different because I didn't expect it would take such a drastic turn.

Well, now. Wait a minute. Come to think of it, I did get warnings that something was bound to happen. However, as naive as I was throughout my marriage, I ignored not only the warning signs but the bells, whistles, and blaring alarms the entire time.

Okay, okay. Before I go into all of that, allow me to give you a high-level overview of "him,"; my now ex-husband who I will call "Reggie" from this point forward, and give you a few tad-bits about our relationship before he betrayed me. I need to be clear for starters, this is not about Reggie although you need to have a little insight about him upfront. As you read through this quick intro, you're probably going to say, "wait a minute, why did you leave out the good stuff?" Don't worry. Trust me; it will all come together in the next section of Him. Because that's who this is all about anyway, right? Now you're getting it. Remember, these the next five chapters will be quick reads to give you a little to nibble on, so don't try to put things together right now. It will all come together after you get further into it, okay? All right.

Let me introduce "him."

How It All Started

Some of us have had that moment when we look at our life and say, "Wow, my life is good right now!" Life is going so well, you feel unstoppable. The wind is to your back, and all you can do at that moment is take a deep breath and smile. Ahhh, there's no better feeling than that. That's how it was for me, but I felt the time had come to make a much-needed change. I needed a new lease on life, and I craved for my environment to change.

I longed to see something different from what I'd seen for the last 40+ years. Perhaps a new city would do the trick.

Now, I have to admit it was a bit scary because I would have never thought I would pack up and moved to a different state EVER. I knew I wanted to relocate to my company headquarters in Dallas for career reasons, so I gathered up the fam (my sons, mom, and brother) and planned a visit to Dallas during my son's spring break. The visit was a huge success. Instantly, I fell in love with the city, and that weekend in Dallas, I decided to move. After a year of planning, I headed to Dallas to take up residency.

I Met "him"

In August 2012, I moved to Dallas. That was the best decision I could have ever made because I finally chose myself. I dared to do something different, and it worked. Ya' girl was living at a whole new level. After a couple of months, I'd settled into my new apartment, got acclimated to my new city, and enjoyed my new state of being an empty-nester, at least for a short time. And I wanted to keep it going.

I'd been in Dallas for roughly six months. It was 2013, a new year, and I was still enjoying my new lease on life. My career was going well, and I made some friends in a short time. I remember sitting in my apartment one afternoon. The weather was picture perfect, and all was well. Then, it dawned on me I'd developed a simple routine of going to work, to the store, and home. Boring! I wanted to do something different. I needed to meet some new people. I thought, *maybe it was time for me to date again and perhaps even settle down with a nice guy*. Life was good, and I realized that it was long overdue for some "me time."

After much consideration (oh, about three days), I decided to give online dating a try. I wasted no time in setting up my online profile, and, immediately, I started getting notifications. Okay, wait a minute. Yes, I know, I know. I can hear you all saying, "You're supposed to wait on God to send you a man." Well, I didn't. Okay? Are we good now? All right.

Right after I completed my profile, I started getting notifications. I sat thumbing through them all. It went a little something like this; Scroll...(Nah). Scroll...(nope). Hum...(like). Scroll.... (oh hell'z naw).

Look, let me tell you, I knew I'd had enough of that mess after so many times of doing that. I mean, yes, I had a few messages and conversations, but they fell off quickly. "Chil', you funny; why did you sign up then?" Point taken, but that particular day, I was done.

One day while online, I got a "ping" from a guy named Reggie. His message said, "I like your profile, and you're nice looking too." I immediately went to his profile and thought, *Eh... he's all right*. He wasn't my type per se, but no harm in striking up a conversation. So, what the heck; I responded. We started off exchanging niceties for a brief moment; then, I stopped responding. The next thing I knew, he pinged me with his number and asked me to give him a call. I said, "okay," but I never did. A couple of days later, I was online again, and another ping from the same guy asking when I would call ("You said you were gonna call; whassup?"). Humph, I thought he was a little forward, and I'd call another time, but he kept with the dang pinging. So, of course, I called.

Our first conversation was quite surprising because we had an instant connection. We laughed with and at each other from the start. We talked about ourselves, you know, the usual stuff: where you from, where you live, where you work, you got any kids....yadda yadda yadda. It was a great conversation, and it seemed like we hit it off. So, I agreed to keep in touch, but I was determined to keep "my plan" in place and not allow Reggie to see me right away. Wait, what plan? My bad. I had a plan that I wouldn't let the guy see me in person for a few months until we got to know each other better during this online dating experience. Got it? Okay. I explained the plan to Reggie. I asked if he was up to the task. To my surprise, he agreed. Don't you love it when things work out just the way you planned them? I know I do.

Now that my "plan" was in action, we began talking regularly, every morning on our way to work, during the day sometimes, and, of course, after work. That was our routine every day for about 45 days straight. It was a breath of fresh air because there wasn't a topic we didn't discuss. We talked about family, backgrounds, and how our parents raised us growing up, our experiences in life, our children, and our goals. You name it; we talked about it. We even talked about our spiritual walk and the things that brought us to the point we were in life. I remember telling Reggie how important it was to me for the guy I could be interested in to have the same spiritual beliefs. He agreed. Right away, we started talking about God. As time went on, I became more comfortable with him and our conversations. I felt he was genuine and authentic.

After a few more weeks of talking on the phone, I decided that I was ready to meet Reggie face-to-face. I was two weeks shy of the three months, but hey, things seemed to be going so well. What can a couple of weeks hurt, right? Well, we agreed to have our first date. Let me put you in on something. We only had pictures of each other via text. So, I was a little nervous. Do you know that show *Catfished*? Now, don't think a sister wasn't tripping 'cause she was. I was about to talk myself out of it, but then I had to tell myself to calm down. I was excited to finally meet. We decided to meet at a restaurant close to where I lived. I arrived first and waited for about 15 minutes. My focus was on the other side of the restaurant. I recognized Reggie as he walked in. I sat and watched until he noticed me. Eyes were locked on each other, right. Then he did what I like to call the "Awwwwe damn, Gina" thing. Got dang it, he did something a man should never do. Please wait for it. He waved me over.

I'm talking about that country wave with his arm all up in the air waving. So, there I was, rolling my eyes so hard. I thought, *Really? This how we're doing this?* Now, me being me to the core, I gave it right back. I waved for him to come to me. He walked toward me. He had this huge grin on his face. The look I had on my face was screaming, "Bruh, you just got your first strike." Then I asked, "Uhm, did you just wave me over to you?"

He looked as if I had two heads and asked, "Yeah, what's wrong with that?"

I said, "Tell me what's right about you waving all countryfied in this restaurant like you ain't got no sense."

He just fell out laughing. When he noticed I wasn't laughing, he said he just saw me and motioned for me to come over to him and didn't mean any disrespect by his actions.

Humph. Okay, maybe he was comfortable because of all the conversations we had before seeing one another. Perhaps a little too damn comfortable.

As the date continued, we sat at the restaurant bar and picked up right where we left off from our phone conversations. It was easy because we already knew enough about each other for it not to be forced. We had a great first date. I could tell I was feeling myself a couple of weeks after that date. I took pride in knowing that "my" plan was working. I wasn't tripped up on life because everything was good, and I enjoyed spending time with him. Later, we discussed how things were between us and agreed that we were on the same page and ready to enter into an exclusive relationship. After a few more discussions, we set boundaries (at least I thought). We both were officially off the market and the dating app.

Things were going well, and we enjoyed ourselves together. He looked me in the eye when we talked and was very attentive. He sent me poems and flowers regularly. We were hanging out all the time. I honestly thought this online dating thing would be a big bust due to the horror stories I'd heard. But that wasn't the case for me. I guess I got lucky. Time went on, and we started getting into a rhythm now. We'd shared our feelings and were able to talk through things we felt needed to be addressed and landed in a suitable place from each discussion. All in all, we had a good thing going.

I think it's safe to say that we all compare at some point in our relationships. We compare the new relationship to the past ones. We compare the things our parents, mentors, or friends have told us about relationships to see if they measure up. We even compare the relationship to what God says in His Word. I know I did. I needed to stay true to my beliefs and relationship with God when it came to a serious relationship. God tells us, "Do not be yoked together with unbelievers" (2 Cor 6:14). So where was He in all this?

Gotta Put God in It

My relationship with God was important to me. I grew up in the church. At a young age, I accepted Jesus as my Lord and Savior, and I knew He would be an essential part of my life for the rest of my life.

I've seen God's hand at work in my life and experienced some situations only He could rescue me from; and He did. I did everything I could to grow my relationship with Him, and it wouldn't be any different for my relationships because I desired to be with a man who had the same beliefs as a Christian.

Early on in our dating relationship, I shared with Reggie how important this was for me, and he accepted it wholeheartedly. We shared our spiritual experiences of accepting Christ and had different stories about how evident God was in our lives. It made me feel good not only to know that I was with someone who believed the same thing I believed spiritually but also wasn't afraid to talk about God. Trust me; it makes all the difference.

After we were officially a couple, we started attending church together. Let me pause and express how romantic it is for a man to attend church with his girlfriend in the early stages. Now, I'm not labeling guys, but it's rare to find. It's even more romantic when you can talk to your man about the sermon, the lessons revealed, and how to be doers of His Word. That's right; we did all this on the ride home. Chil', you talk about red hearts in the eyes. Yep, that was me. Seriously, it was so refreshing to talk about God and get to know this man at the same time. Now, I said I was going to be real with this. So, as naivety would kick in as it does when it comes to heart matters, I have to confess, he had me by the fourth time we attended together. I'm just saying, it's the truth. That was me, ya'll. I loved the Lord, and now I had a guy that was right there with me. Chil', Pa-lease.

One Sunday, he and I attended church with one of my girlfriends. The sermon was about Joseph and his brothers and how they sold him into slavery. And what a powerful sermon it was. Every so often, I would look over at Reggie. I could tell something was going on. The look on his face was intense, as if there were a lump in his throat. His eyes were blinking fast. He tried as best he could to suppress whatever emotions he felt, but I knew the Holy Spirit was working all up and through him because the sermon was so profound. On the ride home after service, we started discussing the sermon, as always. He was asking questions, and, of course, we started discussing the sermon in depth. No shade, but we both knew that I had a deeper understanding of the Word, so he was throwing the questions out there. My friend was crying in the back seat. It was as if we were having an extended service on the way home.

We arrived back at my apartment. In the other room, I talked with my friend about everything from the sermon on how good God was to unpack His message for us. It was quite relevant to what we all were going through on some level or another. As we were talking (and crying), I heard Reggie call me. As I approached the room, I saw him sitting on the bed's edge with a look of desperation and concern on his face. He asked if I would pray for him and, immediately, I agreed, but I wasn't sure what to pray for. I asked what was going on. He responded, "I'm just tired of the way my life is." He kept saying it over and over again. Then I noticed the tears rolling down his face. He just hung his head down and said again that he was tired.

I stood next to Reggie for a few seconds and started telling God thanks. I repeated this a few times as I began to pray. Something was happening. There was a spirit of heaviness around me, so I prayed more. As I began to speak against the enemy, I also prayed that God would open Reggie's heart to accept all that He had for him and release him from anything that was against him. I asked God to reveal His will to him and for Reggie to have a heart for God. I asked God to cover his life, give him favor and strengthen him to be the man he created. I thanked God for covering his life. After a few minutes of praying, I began to let go as he cried harder. Then it went into a soft sobbing like sound. My heart broke for Reggie but I knew, somehow, he would be all right as we embraced each other.

Prayer works. Can I repeat it? Did you hear me? I said, Prayer works! God tells us, "For wherever two or three come together in honor of my name; I am right there with them! Matt 18:20 (TPT). Have you ever prayed for someone, and it was so intense you knew that prayer got answered? Now, wait just a minute. I'm not saying that God was on my timetable, and bam, like a magic wand, waved, the prayer sealed. Not at all. Matt 9:29b-TPT version says, "You will have what your faith expects!" For what do you have faith? What do you expect from God as you honor him with your requests? When Reggie asked me to pray for him, I could tell he was desperate. So, I approached God humbly but boldly and with authority given to me through Jesus Christ to receive what he was seeking after (Hebrews 4:16-TPT). I knew he was free from whatever it was that troubled him. That day the connection he and I had through prayer would forever seal and lay the foundation I needed to pray for him.

A couple of weeks later, I was preparing for our annual cousin's trip to Branson, Missouri Fourth of July weekend. Arriving at the resort and just about ready to settle in, Reggie called. He was so elated because he'd finally received a favorable business notice that would help him tremendously. He said he'd finally gotten his freedom. It was ironic that he said that because the day he called me was the Fourth of July. He recognized his freedom, and God heard his prayer. It made me fall in love with Reggie even more. His confidence in God helping him was inspiring.

Later, arriving home from my vacation, he picked me up from the airport. When I got in the car, he had a huge smile on his face. I could sense a lighter presence about Reggie. Over the weekend, I had thought about him saying the word "freedom," and I saw it radiate from his face. It did me some good to see that he was so happy, and I was so excited about what was to come between us.

What Signs?

Warnings. Why are warnings necessary to heed? You probably know that they mean there could be harm or danger ahead. Or maybe there's something we need to give notice to that could make for an unpleasant situation. I would venture to add that warnings serve as reminders, and most are big fat stop signs that you better not run through or else there will be consequences. So why then do we overlook them or even ignore them? Undoubtedly, the signs are there.

For example, the red heated coil on a stovetop is a clear sign for you to notice the stove is on, and you'll get burned if you touch it. A parent will tell their child to stay back if headed toward danger. In the same vein, we've all seen the warning sign that reads, "Enter at your own risk." We understand that to mean, if you proceed forward, you're taking on the risk of anything happening that you didn't expect and implies a degree of harm. Therefore, warning signs are vital, and we should acknowledge them, even though we often don't.

It's no difference in relationships. The warning is in the pit of our stomach and stays most times until the issue resolves. For me, I call it my "knower." Others call it instinct, gut feeling, or inner man. We get that feeling inside where we're sure about something. I believe it's a vital part of each of us, and it's there for a purpose: to protect, guide, and alert us. May I suggest that most of us have times when we second guess the knower in us?

Now, to drive this home even more resonant, I have to put some God on it. Jeremiah 6:10 (MSG) says, "I've got something to say. Is anybody listening? I have a warning to post. Will anyone notice? It's hopeless! Their ears are stuffed with wax—deaf as a post, blind as a bat." Okay, Whoa! Seriously. Are we that hellbent on ignoring the signs only to, as in my case, stick to the "plan"?

Extra-curricular Activity Sign

During our "couple-ship," I paid attention to the things Reggie would do and say. He was an avid golfer, which I didn't mind. For the most part, he would schedule his golf outings when it didn't interfere with us. However, after a while, this began to change. More and more, he would make golf the priority, and we would get together "after" golf. At first, I didn't say much about it, until it became apparent that whatever we did as a couple had to come after his game of golf. At times, I would plan something ahead of time, and he'd agree to go. However, when the time came, he would say it had to wait until he finished golfing. Our first little spat was about him golfing after I already planned a date for us before he scheduled his tee-time. I asked him to be considerate of our preplanned time together. In turn, he kindly reminded me that he was golfing before he met me and would continue to do so.

Hum, mmkay. I wasn't expecting that response, but I let it slide. No biggie. Well, the no biggie started to turn into a yes biggie. The inconsideration went on for a while and eventually stayed. While his actions didn't sit well with me, I didn't want something insignificant like golf to come between us. So, I ignored the small warning signs, and we went onward in the relationship.

We all have moments when we sense something is off-kilter. It might be a little gut punch. C'mon, be honest, we all have them. It rises a bit, causing an alarm to go off. But what do we do most times? We shrug it off. We dismissed it as "Oh, that's not a big deal." And that, my dear friend, is when you start getting stuck when you fail to take action (knowing you should have done or said something). It doesn't matter how big or small. If it's a deal, it's a big deal, so pay attention to it. It won't go away or fix itself. No. I'm sorry it doesn't work that way, and it sure didn't work that way for me. I ignored more of the warning signs, and I paid a high price for it. Most of us know after you take the bait and get caught up, that's when the person you thought was real leaves the scene. We sometimes refer to them as "representatives." After a while, Honey, and I do mean a short while, the referee taps them out as if they're in a wrestling match, and the real one takes over. And damn it, in most situations, it's too late. But I'll get more into that later.

Money Sign

I started noticing more characteristics and behaviors in Reggie that I hadn't seen in the beginning. You know disguised flaws usually appear when normalcy sets in and you let your guard down. Well, I noticed he had a thing with money. I know; there's nothing wrong with wanting money. But this was different. He was what I like to now call "scheme beaming" on how to get money. He was all over the place with business ideas, where the money would come from, and how to get around to make it easier. I knew early on he was thinking of starting a business. Yes, he also shared with me that he didn't have much growing up. So, I understood his fixation with money. He told me he was building his money back up and didn't have much to "offer" me, but I wasn't looking for Reggie to offer me anything because I had my own and could take care of myself. However, the mistake I know I made was being too transparent about what I'd built over the years.

We had several conversations about money, my money, that is. During a conversation we had about getting an eyeglass business started, I recall asking, "What if you had someone who would be willing to help you?" From my perspective, that wasn't an invitation from me; it was just a question. But somehow or another, he took that to mean I was the "someone." Granted, we had some conversations about the importance of having someone in your corner to provide that level of support, but you need to have the foundation to start building.

A couple of weeks later, Reggie asked for $1,500 to "get his credit straight." I told him no. Moreover, we hadn't been together long enough for him to ask me for $1,500." He immediately got mad and said, "If you can't be down with what I'm trying to do, then I'm out." And out the door he went. A couple of days later, I called him to talk about what happened and see where we were going with the relationship. We agreed to let things go, but we just brushed the issue under the rug. Although it was our first argument about my money, it surely wouldn't be the last.

Unsurprisingly, a few months later, I needed to pull some money out of my 401k. Reggie asked if I would pull out an extra $1,500 to help him. Now mind you, we just had the blow-up earlier regarding money, and now we're back at square one as if my answer would be different. It was still no. During the argument, he said I was bragging about how much money I had, and because I was his woman, I should have been willing to support him. For the second time, I told him no. I wasn't concerned with what he needed. He downplayed my response, but I could tell he was pissed. Guess I overlooked the signs because not only did I have a golfing issue, I'd have to deal with a money issue too.

The Sign of a Con

As our relationship progressed, I found that Reggie and I argued about the small stuff. Things that were important for me weren't for him and vice versa. Things got a little bit heated during another argument about golf and his not giving me any attention. I asked him to leave, since it started to escalate, and if he didn't, I would call the police. Why oh why did I say that? He hit the roof. As the situation progressed, I called the police. When I spoke with the dispatcher, Reggie was pacing the living room, yelling that I cut him. What he didn't know was I had the video recording everything. Consequently, he kept up the facade as I continued to record the entire incident. It was quite entertaining to see him pace back and forth, shouting a bunch of bull-skippy and lies.

The dispatcher asked if I had cut him. I repeatedly denied it, but they had to document the allegation that I had a knife or weapon. When the police arrived, they came directly toward me as if they were going to arrest me. What shocked me was that Reggie kept his "act" going until the police moved him outside.

I showed the officer the video. He was shocked and mad. He told me they had every intention of arresting me because there was an alleged weapon involved in the report. As it turns out, after the officers spoke to one another, they were ready to arrest Reggie for making false accusations and told him there was evidence via video. His face hit the floor. They asked if I wanted to press charges, and, of course, I said no. I just wanted him to leave.

I thought about what transpired after they all left. What kind of a person would intentionally accuse someone of something so false without considering the potential fallout? Reggie didn't think about what could happen to me, especially me going to jail. Then it hit me hard. I was in Texas by myself, with no family. Had I been arrested, who would have bailed me out? WOW! He didn't stop to think about that while aiming for his Golden Globe Award for Best Leading Actor.

Well, I'll be damn, I thought as I sat there, shaking my head and tears rolling down my face. But, here's the sad part. And I know it's sad, so don't judge me. I didn't talk to Reggie for days. He continued to call until I gave in and answered. Honestly, I didn't want to hear what he had to say, but I listened. May I add, he never said he was sorry during the conversation. He tried to justify his role-play actions by saying he had to defend himself because they typically take the man to jail without cause. He never considered the breadth of what he did and never took ownership of them.

I'm sure you're wondering if I took him back. The answer is, yes, I took Reggie back. I know, I know. I completely ignored my "knower." But am I the only one? I know I'm in good company with the take-back syndrome, ladies. Oh, I almost forgot this was about me, Urgh. Okay, I swept the whole thing under the rug.

Not to make an excuse, but I wanted to believe there were other good qualities about Reggie. Or, how about we were still getting to know each other, and we hadn't figured out one another's trigger buttons. How about those for good old explanations? Ha! You're not buying it either. Let's call it what it was, excuses. I made excuses for his behavior, skipped right on over that gut feeling, and gave him another chance.

May I offer some sage advice? You cannot or shouldn't overlook when people show you who they are. We've all heard the statement before, and it's a true statement. Isn't it amazing how we so long to be in a relationship that, sometimes, we brush ugly behaviors under the rug? Well, let me say that it has the potential to cause much hardship down the road. At the time, we don't think it's a big deal. But, when we observe them and fail to address them, they can pile up and become problems we would have never wanted.

Because I let Reggie's behavior go unchecked, he hit the repeat button, and they showed up somewhere else later down the road. When we had a blow-up, he would come back around with some sweet sauce to convinced me that it was just a little incident. It was a vicious cycle of arguing then back to being in a better place. Later, something else will pop off, and then we go back to being cool with each other. On and on and over and over again.

Let me help you if I may. Please get off that ride with that person. Give the ticket back and stand in line for one that won't make you sick (sick and tired of being sick and tired).

CHAPTER TWO

Hand in Marriage

The "M" Word

I think most of us can agree that at a very young age, most girls dream about getting married or what their wedding day would be. They even create fantasies during tea parties. They dream. They create. They wonder. And they "plan" that special day in their minds and act it out in private playtimes. Everything is perfect in our imagination. We're happy and already in love. What? Yes, we're in love with a fantasy, a dream, or hope of what could be our picture-perfect future wedding day. We've created visions of the perfect wedding dress and all the frills that come along with it. In our minds, we're engrossed in a wonderland of love and bliss. Nothing could be perfect than that special day.

Where did this grand marriage idea come, especially at such a young age? Perhaps we attended a wedding before with our family members. Or maybe we were designated as the flower girl at a wedding and thought it was the coolest thing ever to walk down the aisle in our pretty dress and everyone sighing the oooh's and ahhh's that made us feel special. It could be we've read it in a children's book. The pictures help us dream of our big day... one day. Whatever the occasion was, we held on tightly to it, and from that moment, started dreaming of our wedding day and how wonderful and happy we would be on that day.

I've been there and done that. Unfortunately, for me, I didn't have that picture-perfect image of marriage, although I had attended a few throughout my life. Not to mention the first time I married, I was young, and it was nothing like I'd dreamed of as a young girl. It was quite the opposite and only lasted a few years. However, that didn't keep me dreaming that I would be married again (after I did some growing up).

Let's be honest; marriage can be somewhat intimidating, especially when you consider the things you may have to give way to, right? We may have to shift our time to include the other. What about sharing personal space? Ladies, please give that man some room in the closet. Sorry, I had to throw that in there. How about our finances? We can't just run out and buy up everything like we used to, hmm? Consider these when you're about to charter into unknown territory, whether you've been married before or not. It's no longer about our being independent or doing things our way. It's about being "other-centered" and not self-centered. And most of all, the relationship should be at the center of everything.

There's something to be said about being able to relinquish control and place your heart in the hands of a person you've decided to trust. Marriage is no small thing to enter into lightly. It takes patience, compromise, and forgiveness daily for marriage to work. Wait. Let me say it differently because I don't care so much about the word "work" regarding marriage. Instead, I think marriage isn't about making it work but you live and give to marriage through patience, compromise, and daily forgiveness. How you live out marriage is visible to everyone who sees you. What you give is what you will likely get back in return. So, if you choose to live and give in marriage with the other being the focus and God at the center, you've got yourself a pretty good thing going.

Before Reggie, I was single for 20 years. I had a couple of relationships, but they didn't change my last name. When I moved to Dallas, I was ready for everything new, including finding someone to fall in love with and, ultimately, get married again.

His Good Thing "GT"

Reggie and I were in a dedicated and exclusive relationship, spending lots of time together. After much deliberation on a career track, he decided to attend a truck driving school and go into business for himself.

I was in girlfriend mode big time. I was having the time of my life. It was refreshing to see Reggie in the grove with trucking. His life was in clear focus because everything he was working toward was for his future entrepreneurship.

Things were serious for real. So serious that we started talking about the "m" word. Yep, marriage. I'll admit, things were moving fast, or shall I say faster than what's considered normal for relationships. But then again, who's to say there has to be a designated amount of time to pass before deciding to take the relationship to the next level? And that's what we did. The more time we spent together, we settled in on this becoming a long-term relationship.

I remember asking Reggie, "Why me?" I wanted to know what it was about me that made him think I was the one for him. He told me that he'd been paying attention to how meticulous I was of my home, the drive I had for my career, how I handled bills and other responsibilities. He told me I would be a good influence for his girls and those were things he looked for in a wife. Honey, when I tell you ya' girl was beaming, do you hear me? I was flattered with everything he said, but it touched me that he even paid attention to those things. Heck, I was doing what I do. I had no idea he paid attention.

Over time, we had deep conversations about marriage and what it meant for him, me, and us together. We were already living together by now. We talked about the finances, spending time together, keeping God in our relationship, and much more. We talked about what marriage would be like "this" time around, since we'd both married before.

Now don't get me wrong. I wasn't about to go out and pick a ring (just yet). My life was what I considered to be a blessing. I'd done all that I wanted to do career-wise, along with raising my sons. I knew I wanted to be a wife again. But not just any ol' wife. I wanted to be a "GT" wife to a good man. You know, a "good thing" (Proverbs 18:22). My heart intentions were 100% pure. I knew I could be a supportive, loving, and submissive wife because I knew I would place God in my relationship. From the very beginning, I put God first and prayed for my future husband and his heart's desires and blessing upon our union. I prayed these prayers before dating because I desired to be a wife. Since I decided I was ready to be married again, it was time to talk with my family.

Blessings Granted

How do you know when you're ready to have "the talk"? I mean we have "the talk" for just about everything. When we're younger, we have the talk to discuss boy's and girl's body parts and the birds and the bees (really, parents, it's called SEX). As we get older, some have the talk with parents about getting our driver's license, buying our first car, and about dating. OMG. You get my drift; we just talk and talk and talk. And let's not forget, as adults, we talk about our careers, buying a house, and, ultimately, while dating, we have to have the "marriage talk." Well, mainly, the women more so than the men. Whew! We've been talking all our lives, right? LOL. But seriously, being in a relationship, it should be expected we will have "the talk" about marriage somewhere down the line. That is, if the relationship is headed in the direction of long-term.

Let me move this story along here. When Reggie and I were dating, I didn't share much about it with my sons. I wanted to give it some time to see how things were coming along before I made introductions. I remember my sons came to Dallas about a year after we had been dating. They hadn't met Reggie yet, but they knew I was dating someone. While they were there, he and the boys hung out together to get to know them. A few weeks later, my best friend came to Dallas. Reggie gets a bright idea to go to the mall. She was all for it, but their excitement was a little too much. I thought, Okay, you're doing too much for wanting to go to the mall. Then she winked at me.

I had no clue what the two of them were up to, but I kept getting separated from them for some strange reason. When I finally caught up with Reggie and Bev in a jewelry store, I asked what they'd been doing. They both brushed me off, but there was something suspicious about the whole thing. Nevertheless, I let it go. Later, my best friend told me he was getting her blessing and opinion on what kind of ring he should be looking for when the time came to buy one for me. The funny thing was that she kept telling him not to get the ring from the mall. That's what BFFs do. I later found out that he wanted to spend time with my sons and talk with them to ask for my hand in marriage. He got their blessing.

I was pleased he put in the time and effort to reach out to my sons and my best friend to include them in his intentions to bring them into the marriage preparations. He made sure that I had a ring that I would like, which made me appreciate his thoughtfulness and carefulness in doing all the things he did to include the people who meant the most to me. Despite everything that took place before preparing or even discussing marriage, he had a heart of compassion, and I knew that he wanted to do everything he could to make me happy.

Home Sweet Home?

Trucking school was coming along very well for Reggie. I was deep in wedding idea mode, but also focused on buying a house. My youngest son would relocate to Dallas after graduation, and I really wanted to close before he arrived. I put in some work and was in full swing setting appointments for Reggie and me to view properties when he came home. He knew how serious I was, but I could tell he was only halfway in on the process for some reason or another. He wasn't as enthusiastic about the whole idea and didn't participate as much either, although I did everything I could to make sure he felt included. I asked him what was going on. Then he hit me with the one-two punch. He said he didn't have any money to buy a house right now, so I would have to do it alone. Uhhhh, okay (eyes rolling). It wasn't what he said. It was how he said it. His tone was defensive, and he was adamant he couldn't contribute. Although I wanted him to participate, I couldn't focus on what he couldn't do financially to stop what I had to do. You've heard it before, "One monkey doesn't stop the show."

What had me puzzled was that I thought we were working toward something (together); therefore, I didn't understand why he would isolate himself from being part of a huge decision that would benefit both of us. Honestly, it was quite sad that, since he felt he couldn't contribute, he couldn't participate in our future in other ways. I had high hopes for us to do things together in our relationship, and it took a turn as he continued to look at his lack of funds instead of what he could contribute. It didn't make sense to me, but I rolled right along with what he said.

I asked Reggie if there was anything he could do, since we were in it together. His response was, "Naw, I don't have anything right now." So, I left it alone. My finances were enough, and I didn't need his. My goal was to buy a house and work the rest out later. Once I get a plan in motion, I move forward. I was used to doing things for myself, and this case was no different. He would contribute after truck driving school, and we would be fine.

After letting that conversation go, the search began. A few weeks later, my agent showed me a few houses. The last day she was in town, she set up a viewing, and when we drove up, I knew it was the one. It had everything on my list, and it was a 4-minute drive from the church. But here's the one thing that took me over the top. The address was 314. Ha! St. Louis area code. I'm from St, Louis. Get it? I know, too much, right?

But seriously, there are no coincidences with God. I was sure every detail of my life continued to weave together to fit into God's perfect plan of bringing good into my life (Romans 8:28 TPT).

It was exciting because I had my sights set on this new lease on life and this new relationship that we were embarking upon. I was even more excited to get everything set up in its proper place for him while he was on the road so that when he came home, he would have a comfortable and spacious place for us to be together.

I shared the house's details with Reggie one day, and when he came home from over-the-road training, we scheduled one last walk-through of the house. As he walked through the house, I watched his facial expressions. I gathered he was a little uncomfortable and disconnected since he didn't participate in the process. Watching Reggie, I used the words "we" and "us" to assure him this would be his home regardless of who had the financial backing for the house. After the walk-through, I asked Reggie his thoughts about the house. He was pleased and said it was a good house for us.

I put a contract and closed on the house just as I knew I would. Closing day was exciting but somber because Reggie wasn't there with me to share in the moment of our new house because he was back on the road. So, I finished the move myself.

I Do. (I Think). I Did.

In March 2014, Reggie and I decided to take some time for a weekend trip to my home in St. Louis, and I was excited for my relatives to meet him for the first time. When we arrived at my mom's house, there was much whispering going on, but I didn't know about what. Later that afternoon, we went to lunch with my dad. Before leaving, my dad and Reggie went off to the side to talk as I sat in the car. When they'd finished, I tried to be nosey and asked what they discussed. Reggie gave me a random answer that didn't make much sense, so I left it alone.

Later that day, we made plans to meet up over at my cousin TT's house for game night, a tradition we have when family come in from out of town. My cousins and brother would be home, which was sure to be a fun-filled weekend. At my cousin's house, women were cooking, music was playing, and kids were running around having a great time. Suddenly, my cousin Tre said they were making a run to the store and beckoned Reggie to go along. I was nervous because if anyone knows my cousin Tre, they'll agree he's a complete fool, just absolutely fun and crazy. I knew he would take any opportunity to "break him in" Reggie into the family. Nonetheless, they left and were gone for quite a while.

After Reggie and my cousins returned, we all ate, and then it was time for the family game to start. The decision was we would play a game called "Mafia." I noticed Reggie had a weird look on his face. He and my cousin Tre were drinking and laughing under their breath. But I just shrugged it off and continued to enjoy my family.

My cousin Pam walked us through the instructions, gave everyone their roles, and told the "town" to sleep. During the moment of silence, I could hear some movement around me but couldn't tell what was going on. She then tells the town to wake up. As I lifted my head from the table and opened my eyes, everyone looked at me, and I mean everybody.

I asked, "What now?" My family stared at me, smiling and laughing; I didn't know what the heck was going on.

"Do you see anything in front of you?" Pam asked. I looked around and straight ahead and replied, "No." She asked again, but this time, she emphasized "in front" of you. I looked around again, not noticing anything. She got into a tizzy and told the town to go back to sleep.

I heard everyone murmuring and snickering as I put my head back down. After a brief moment, she had us wake up. Again, all eyes were on me. I still hadn't caught on to what was happening. Everyone yelled unanimously, "Rho look in front of you." As I glanced down in front of me, I saw a jewelry box. I turned toward Reggie. He was down on one knee. I cupped my hands over my mouth, trying hard not to scream with excitement. When I looked at Reggie, he had the biggest smile on his face. I looked around at everyone in the room, and they were jumping and screaming. All I could do was cry. It was the best surprise I could have ever expected. Then he slipped the ring on my finger, confessed his love for me, and asked if I would marry him. I couldn't get out the word "yes" because I was still in shock and overwhelmed with happiness. Everyone shouted for me to say yes. I told him, yes, and he stood up and hugged me so tight, all I could do was cry.

Listen. Let me tell you about this ring. It was beautiful. It was a 3-carat ring with baguette diamonds around the band and a princess cut smack dab in the middle. It was gorgeous. Everything started to make sense. When the boys and my best friend came to Dallas, he got their blessing and my bestie helped him with the ring selection. After he proposed, I found out that he had been planning the trip to St. Louis months earlier. It never dawned on me that everyone just so happened to be at home in STL on the same weekend. Reggie enlisted my cousin Tre to get everyone to come home to STL that particular weekend for the proposal. Oh, and the conversation he had with my dad? Yep, he asked for my hand in marriage, and my dad said yes. Obviously, we didn't finish playing because the intent was to get me to go to sleep so he could propose. WOW! I couldn't have asked for a better proposal than that.

Wedding Planning

There was a very noticeable shift in Reggie's demeanor after he proposed. His spirit was lighter than before, and he gave me all his attention. The rough times we had before were now in the past, and we were enjoying each other again. We laughed more and spent time together. Now that we'd moved into the house and were settling in comfortably, that was one thing off the list for us. The next thing after the proposal was to focus on planning our wedding.

I had so many thoughts of what I wanted our wedding to be like, and I knew that I had to get started planning, since it was a few months after Reggie's proposal. I felt excited but it seemed as if I didn't have enough time to get everything done between work and supporting him. I was spinning around like plate on a stand from all the planning that needed to happen. I had to get everything down on paper so nothing would be missed. So, I pulled up an Excel spreadsheet and started creating columns and lists. Oh, I wish you could have seen me as I laid out all the ideas that were in my head. I worked hard to take the vision and put it all on paper because I knew this would be one of the most fun and exciting moments in our relationship. But... Reggie was still over the road most times, so, of course, I did most of the planning with my mom's and best friend's help. I gave him updates on how the wedding planning was coming together. I appreciated that he trusted me with it all. He knew I wouldn't go overboard with wedding expenses.

I mentioned earlier that one of his favorite things to do was golfing, and I thought it would be appropriate for us to get married on the golf course. When I shared this idea with him, his eyes lit up and he was on board 100%. We sought out a golf course here in Dallas that was actually one that he frequented. Reggie suggested we visit the golf course and talk to one of the planners. Upon our arrival at the golf course, I could see the look of excitement all over his face, and he was even engaged in the conversation about how the wedding would take place. The wedding planner gave us a tour and how the layout could be according to the number of invitees. Everything seem to be lining up, and it was game on (no pun intended).

While planning and completing the guest list, it dawned on me that most of the wedding guests were in St. Louis. Reggie's family would attend but it wasn't as large as mine. After much consideration, I had the idea to change the location from Dallas to St. Louis. I told him I'd done some research on venues and caterers which would reduce the cost in half if we changed it to St. Louis, to which he gladly agreed.

I know that I wanted my venue to be something different outside of your normal church wedding ceremony or conference hall reception, so I had to call in the cavalry. And by "the cavalry," I mean my brother. He knows every venue in St. Louis that would give my special day that sense of beauty and elegance I wanted. After speaking with him, I was bombarded with options. Let me say that my brother and I are somewhat alike because we both have the spirit of "takeover." He sent pictures, outlined wedding packages, did comparisons, and the whole bit. Whew! I thought I was a planner. But it was very much appreciated because he's a little (lot) bougie, so I knew it was going to be fabulous.

After much consideration, we decided on The Third-Degree Glass Factory. We would be able to create an experience not only for ourselves but for our guests as well, with glass blowing as an interactive part of the wedding. The wedding would be surrounded by unique pieces of glass blown art with vibrant colors throughout the space along with an urban gallery of artistic design all around it. It was the perfect place to make our wedding day one Reggie and I would never forget.

It was time for me to bring my best friend and mom in to close out the planning. My best friend helped me secure the cake baker and caterer, while my mom made connections with the decorator, and they both set up viewings and tastings for me. The only thing left for me was to take a trip back home to taste them myself. When I arrived at the bakery, my choices had been narrowed down to sample six flavors. Listen....when I tell you the samples tasted amazing. I decided to do a top tier cake and the other three tiers were cake pops on them instead of the traditional wedding cake style. I also knew most people would eat a smaller piece of cake instead of a slice. Trust me; I wasn't about to throw away money on uneaten cake.

So now, the last thing I needed to take care of was the food. Let me stop right here. I have been to a few weddings where the food was horrible. A funny thing about weddings is that, while they're someone's special day, you don't ever forget what was bad about them, right. I wasn't about to have anyone speaking disparagingly about my wedding food...at all. I'll admit my wedding day was all about me. But I also wanted the experience to be memorable for my friends and family. When I thought about how they would remember my wedding, I wanted them to think engaging. When it came to the food, I had flashbacks of the traditional sit-down dinner with china plates and elegant silverware. Yep, all good and dandy, but not for me. I wanted people to mingle with us and each other. The venue was set up with a baked potato bar, burger bar, finger foods bar, fruit bar, and salad and soup bar stationed in different areas around the room. The guests could serve themselves and continue to mingle throughout the reception.

I'd made final selections for the wedding colors, caterer, decorator, venue (thanks to my brother), closed out the invitation list for our guests, set up the website, and picked out the ladies' dresses and mine, of course. Whew. And I did it all within 3 months. My mom, brother, and best friend made the process seamless after we decided to hold the wedding in St. Louis.

A couple of weeks before the wedding, my dress finally arrived. I didn't want a full-length wedding gown, so, instead, I had a three-quarter length dress embellished with lace flowers, a silk net and silk wide cummerbund that puffed out. When it came, I was nervous about trying it on but also excited at the same time. I hid the dress in the closet out of his sight. When I put the dress on, it fit like a glove. I felt beautiful, and I hadn't even walked toward the mirror yet. The stitching was perfect with every detail elegantly done. I smiled so hard my cheeks started to hurt. As I stood in front of a full-length mirror and saw myself in the dress, emotions came rushing in like a mighty flood. I couldn't stop the tears from falling down my face. This dress was it and I was absolutely stunning. Flashes of my wedding day raced through my head, and all I could do was smile. I couldn't wait for the day to be his wife, especially in this dress.

After standing in the mirror for what seemed like forever, I blew a kiss at myself, shot myself a wink, and told myself, "You got this one in the bag, honey." I won't lie, I even took a whirl around the hallway in the dress so I could see how it would flow when I danced, strutted, and walked. Yes, Chil', I was feeling myself and all that and a bag of chips, and I couldn't wait for him to see me in a few weeks.

All in all, I had everything confirmed. All that was left was to prepare to go into this life of being married together. All things came together, and I still had a few months before the wedding the following April to relax and focus on him. When ya' girl gets to planning, she gets it done ahead of schedule because she doesn't like surprises (she's a little perfectionist. Yes, she is).

The Marriage Gut Check

Let's fast-forward a bit. The wedding week had finally arrived, and I was back home in St. Louis, ready for the celebrations to begin. Reggie stayed back for a couple more days due to work and would arrive a couple of days before the wedding day.

I could tell I was nervous, but it was a ball of good nerves (I thought). I admit I tend to overthink things a bit. I remember lying in bed that Wednesday before his arrival. I thought of the many ways the wedding and the rest of my life would be going forward. All the "what-ifs" and "what abouts" bombarded my mind. (Psst – that was all the signs I overlooked earlier, giving me one last kick in the gut.) Every argument we'd ever had up until that moment raced through my mind. I revisited the hurtful feelings he caused and the times he wasn't there when I needed him. Practically, every experience we'd had, played like a motion picture on the big screen of my mind. I felt sick. Was this what I truly wanted?

I'm sure you're thinking that wasn't the best time to start questioning myself. But I did. I questioned if Reggie were the right one and if I'd given him too many mess-ups. I questioned if he could provide, protect, or love me how I needed to be loved. Yep, the questions went on and on. The pit of terror was more profound and more in-depth with each critique and with each question. What about his snoring? Could I live with that noise for the rest of my life? Really? Was I actually over the golfing and money issues? Could I handle my husband being away on business, leaving little time for me?

Whew. It was a lot to think about, and it was the absolute wrong time for me to fuss over it at that point. I convinced myself it would be fine, since it was only nerves taking over. Or, was it instinct? Was it a warning? All I knew was Reggie would arrive the next morning, and I needed to settle my mind, as I'd already made the decision for us to get married.

The Big Day

The day had arrived, my wedding day to Reggie. Although I was a ball of nerves, I was so excited to become his wife. All the previous doubts and anxiety somehow washed away, knowing he and I would commit ourselves to each other to a lifetime of love. When I arrived at the venue, everything was picture perfect. Our friends and family were there, and the atmosphere was filled with chatter and laughter. It was a day I'll never forget. I was mostly proud because my dad performed our ceremony (yes, I'm a preacher's kid), and my oldest son walked me down the aisle while my youngest stood beside Reggie. That day, I would marry my lover and my friend.

Once the ceremony began, and I entered the room, I saw Reggie standing there with his arms crossed in front of him and his shoulders back, standing tall and proud. I held onto my son tightly and whispered, "Say something funny to keep me from crying." We both started laughing, and that took away the nervousness as I walk toward Reggie. My friend Jackie and my best friend Beverly were smiling as I walked toward Reggie. And as I reach the end of the aisle, standing right before him, I saw the look on his face, and with tears in his eyes, he smiled at me. I felt his love for me.

We exchanged our vows, words filled with endearments and jokes. We poured blue and beige sand into a round cylinder to symbolize that our lives were infused together from that day forward, April 4. Of course, after the ceremony, we took pictures and then came back to kick off the reception party.

Our wedding day had so much love and happiness, laughter, and joy. Reggie and I were husband and wife. I made a vow to him that he was the only one for me, and then I would love and support him always. I made a vow to God that I would always hold Reggie before Him and be the wife he would teach me to become.

We spent the rest of our special day with family and friends. Oh, but then we had to seal that day with affectionate love, and that we did. Oh, how I didn't want the feeling to end.

Marriage Move Over

I will resolve to say that we've all heard of the saying, "All good things must come to an end." Why is that? Why do good things have to come to an end? Why can't they last and last. With almost everything in life, there's a beginning, and there, indeed, is an end. There's the beginning of the day (morning), and there's an end to the day, what we call night. There's the beginning of life with a child's birth, and then there's death that ends life. We start hungry, and after we've eaten, we're full. And then there are relationships. Most significantly, for me, there were many beginnings and endings in the first two years before marriage. We began and ended the dating phase. We began and ended the argument phase. Well, not really, but you get my drift. We started the marital period that went into the honeymoon phase, and, much to my surprise, that ended pretty darn fast, a little too fast for the kid.

In all honesty, I thought we would be in a state of honeymoon bliss for a while. You know, that phase after marriage where you're so in love you do everything together like washing dishes, folding clothes, or just sitting up with each other watching TV together. It's the phase where you can't take your hands off each other. It's much like, every time you walk by, he pats you on the ass and says to himself, umm, umm, umm. All the while, you're pretending you want him to stop patting that ass. Let's be real. I looked forward to all that and then some.

I dreamed of how it would be to say my new last name. Every chance I got, it rolled off my lip: "Yes, Mrs. Washington. Hi, I'm Mrs. Washington. Oh, I'm sorry I didn't give you my last name (chuckle chuckle); it's Washington. Pa-lease!" You couldn't tell me nothing. I know that's not proper English, but you couldn't tell me NO-thing!! You know why? 'Cause I was Mrs. Washington.

Well, unfortunately for us, we were back to life now. All the glitz and glam from the wedding was over. All the fun times walking on the Vegas strip and staying up all night enjoying our honeymoon ended, over, caput. Now what I had to do as a wife was keeping the big house clean, going to work every day, coming home to start dinner, chit chat for a few minutes with him, and then turn in for bed, only to start it all over the next day. The fact is I loved every moment of it. Even though the fun came to a screeching halt, I was still his wife. I also thought it would be easy for me to juggle because I enjoyed doing it for him. So what if the honeymoon were technically over? He and I were husband and wife, and I looked forward to the "just us phase" for at least the first year. Hmmm, but something interrupted that for me: his business.

CHAPTER THREE

Hands on the Business

Competition is something that pushes us to strive to give our very best. Competition compels us to identify who or what is in the number one position. Whether it's against another person or thing, we'll go hard to obtain the accolades it brings. It's certainly no different in relationships. We fight so they'll notice us. We scream so they can hear us, especially if we feel our voices aren't heard. We even perform outside of our comfort zone to become the most important person in our partner's life. The competition takes a lot of work too. You have to go through vigorous training to compete with the best of the best, not to mention the mental capacity it takes to keep you in the game. But, how do you begin competing with something you had no idea you need to compete with?

Who would ever imagine having to compete with anything in marriage? Yes, there will be something that will take precedence in the relationship, whether it be spending time together, finances, or a host of other things. There will be times when one spouse will make sacrifices for something, and the other will make sacrifices for something else. In either case, sacrifices should result in both of them benefiting in the relationship in the grand scheme of things.

In my case, I had to compete with the business for his time and attention. My husband told me that once he landed on something, he would be locked in, so I completely understood this meant there'd some days ahead where the focus was on getting the business started. It didn't matter to me. I mean, how much time can a person spend on business knowing he had a wife to spend time with as well?

Going Into Business

Upon our honeymoon return, he wasted no time talking about buying equipment to get the business going. Now, I'm not saying that I knew all the ins and outs of starting a business; however, I knew that you had to have a plan, and I hadn't seen or heard Reggie talk of one. When I mentioned it to him, he said, "There you go with all your plans and shit. Sometimes, you have to leap."

I said, "Yep, I get that, but let's get to these questions I have, though." I wasn't trying to be a dream killer, but, my goodness, we were married, and what he did from that moment on would affect me. Look, I was a corporate girl, and I'll admit I conditioned myself to do things decently and in order. Well, that wasn't how he rolled. Reggie was a real risk-taker and had no fear of betting his last on anything he thought was a sure win. He flew by the seat of his pants and danced to his drum. No questions asked, and, for some reason, it chapped my entire ass. It was unnerving to me that he would go, go, go. I'm not wired that way because I calculate risks before jumping in.

As I watched the business consume all of Reggie's time, I didn't say much. I just sat back and observed. That's when I noticed the look in his eye that said, "by any means necessary." He would start this business no matter what it took. Nothing was going to stop him, not even his wife, with all her questions.

Day after day, I watched him working on the business and he was relentless. He stayed online, searching, printing papers, and submitting payments to get the business going. I saw signs of us hitting a brick wall in our communication with each other again. I knew it had everything to do with the focus on the business. The niceties were fading fast, and tempers were running short. I hear you saying, "Give him a break; he's trying to build a business that will benefit you." I get it. I get it. I get it. Yes, his determination to build a business was strong, and I admired him for it. His focus on the business was like a laser, and I loved him for that. Yes, I know all of that. But damn, we were just married six weeks prior, and you mean to tell me that's dust in the wind. That's some Fraggle-nackle bull skippy. I noticed the shift in his focus and attitude; hell, it was apparent. Sure enough, he was all in and was relentless in his pursuit to get the business going no matter what. So, I thought it best if I stayed out of the way. Despite it all, anything he needed, I made sure I was available for him.

Un-Equipped for Business

The business was official. Most times, when we'd come home from work, Reggie would head straight to the computer and stay on until late into the night and all day on the weekends, pricing trucks and trailers.

Most of our conversations were about the business. We no longer talked about us; everything was about the business. During a conversation about equipment, I asked Reggie where he would get the money. He blew it off a little bit but said he'd pull it together and let me know. I continued to ask how he was going to buy the truck. He interrupted and told me not to worry about that; he just needed to know if I was with him.

There I stood, like a deer in the headlights, trying to find the words to respond. But, of course, I said okay, although still confused because I didn't know where the money would come from to fund the business. Now I'm a smart girl. I knew we (he) didn't have money sitting in the bank to start up a business. Something told me that he was going to utilize his credit cards to fund the business...or mine.

A little later, we were talking, and, of course, the business came up. Reggie came out of nowhere and said we needed to buy a truck. He'd been looking at trucks for a few days and landed on a few he wanted to check out. As I listened, I saw the question coming to me before Reggie said a word. Yes, he asked if I could help him buy the truck. Now, wait, wait. I know I said I was all in, and I was. But, before giving him an answer, I had a few questions I needed answers to so we could be on the same page.

I had questions such as "How much do you need? How soon are you thinking about buying? Monthly payment?" I had the "normal" questions any person would ask. Well, hold on, Miss Know-It-All; you're asking too many damn questions. My questions didn't sit well with him, either. Then he hit me with the 1-2-punch. He said, "Forget it. I'll do it myself." Wait! That's how we're going to end the conversation?

As I started to speak, all I could see were the diamonds on his back as he slid out of sight like a snake. I only need a minute to talk, but, nope. He was out of there, and I mean that literally. He grabbed his golf clubs and said he'd be back later.

That wasn't what I expected. At best, I hoped we'd put some of the good ol' communication skills we learned from counseling to work. Nah, it didn't happen. Reggie went into shut down mode, leaving me to figure out what went wrong.

Not too long after that incident, Reggie was excited because he found a truck. Uhhhhh, excuse me, bruh? I wish you had been there to see the look I had on my face. Please understand my surprise. I wasn't aware he was at the point of purchasing a truck yet. We hadn't picked up from the last conversation we had about buying a truck, so I wondered how we got there that quickly. And now, you want to talk. Okay, let's go. Chil', none of that mattered. He wasn't tripping off the look I had on my face. He was Unbothered. He told me we were leaving to go to the sales lot.

At this point, everything was spinning in my head. We'd just gotten back from our honeymoon, and within a matter of weeks, he registered and established a business (without many conversations with me, mind you). We hardly had any time to be married because the business occupied every waking moment of his time. I slowly drifted into the background until he needed something from me: my money. Now, he wanted to take notice of me. Okay. You know what? I'll roll with it. Let's go. I'll show him how a GT does things. I was fired up with excitement for him and frustrated for myself—time to show and prove.

We arrived at the sales lot and looked around at a couple of semis. Boy, oh boy, I could see the excitement all over his face, which made me even more excited for him. We jumped in a rig to take it for a test ride. I was excited for him because I knew this was a dream of his. At that point, I had to let all the foolishness go ('cause I was a hot mess) and support him as much as I possibly could.

After we got back home, we continued talking about purchasing equipment. As we talked about all things trucking, Reggie asked if I was all in with him. Of course, I said yes. He asked if I would put the down payment for the truck on my credit card because he was okay with financing. I must admit it took me by surprise because, before scouting trucks, the marriage was a little touch and go. I had no idea that he would drop that bomb on me again because he still hadn't answered the questions I had regarding the truck.

Be that as it was, I sat there. I felt like he put me on the spot because I really couldn't say no. After all, we'd been to the sales lot for the truck, so I agreed. Later we went back to the dealership to draw up the paperwork. I just said I would support him, and, hopefully, things will turn around and be back in the place where we know that we should be. I whipped out the credit card to make the down payment for the truck.

Reggie had a truck, but he didn't have a trailer yet. I begin to talk with him about the next steps. I brought up the fact that he didn't have the trailer, and when I asked him, to my surprise, he told me that his mom helped him get the trailer. Humph. Is that so? I said to myself. When I asked how that happened, he reminded me that I acted as if I didn't want to give him the money; so, he went to her, and she made it happen.

Now mind you, I wasn't upset by the fact that Reggie's mom helped him purchase the equipment. I was upset by him not telling me anything about it. I felt he went behind my back because he "thought" I wasn't going to help him and didn't tell me anything about it. We were also married, and we should have discussed it as husband and wife and agreed, especially about things that would affect our future. I understood that everything he and I did going forward would directly affect the other, which I expressed to him. When I told him how I felt about the situation going to his mom, he said to me, "Well, you act like you didn't want to be a part of it. I knew I needed to get this business off the ground and running, so I knew I could always count on my mom if I couldn't count on you. I was utterly shocked that he felt he needed to turn to his mom instead of coming to his wife, ready and willing to support him. So, I walked away from the conversation feeling he went behind my back and didn't include me with significant decisions that would impact us as husband and wife.

All About the Business

It was rough in the first few months of being married. It was becoming a regular thing to see the back of Reggie's head as I rode in the business's perpetual back seat. Everything he did was about the business, and I must be honest and admit I felt a little jealous. Okay, a lot. There were many times I threw a temper tantrum behind closed doors because I thought I would have him to myself for a couple of months after being married. However, that wasn't my reality. When we had been dating, I had to compete with golfing to get some time with him, and after marriage, I had to fight with the business for his time. I certainly don't want you to think golfing just disappeared because it didn't. I was competing with a two-headed monster of time, golf and the business, and it seemed as if I were losing big time.

Reggie stayed true to what he wanted to accomplish. Despite some hiccups along the way and how he did things, he started his own trucking business. I wanted to be the supportive and encouraging wife he needed. I committed to providing the financial backing he needed because we were in the marriage together.

During long nights, Reggie sat at the computer, searching load boards for freight. There were also long days with him making back-to-back calls, building business relationships. I watched him intensely. I watched everything he did. I could tell when he was pumped and raring to go, and nothing could stop him. I could also tell when things were taking a toll on him from time to time. I wanted to make sure that I was a "soft" place for him to land at the end of a busy day.

Oh, yeah, I prayed for him. I prayed that God would bless his efforts, and the business would be successful. I remembered the scripture that says, "Before you do anything, put your trust totally in God and not in yourself. Then every plan you make will succeed" (Proverbs 16:3 TPT). The NIV translation merely says, "Commit to the Lord whatever you do, and he will establish your plans." Oh, how desperately I wanted his plans to succeed. Hence, I committed myself to pray for him and keeping him before the Lord. I prayed his finances would be in line with what he needed for the company to grow and asked God to provide him the financial resources he needed. Most of all, I asked Him to change my heart toward how much he worked. I knew I couldn't make this about me. I knew I had to sacrifice to make room for him to be the man he needed to be for me and our future. Nonetheless, he had my support entirely.

But wait. It was starting to become overwhelming for me. I was missing my husband already in our marriage. How was it even possible to miss him so soon after our wedding vows? I mean, seriously, isn't there a time limit law that mandates couples to spend time together after the wedding/honeymoon for at least six months without interruption. Okay, I'm asking for too much. There's no such law. Maybe that was my plan or expectation. I'll admit that, especially when I revisited past moments with him in my mind. Couldn't he have waited a little while to start the business? What if, what if, what if. That's all I had.

Funding the Business Ain't Fun'd

Funding a business cost money. Period. Point blank. Considering where those resources will come from is all too important to rush through. Thinking it through instead of assuming it will be fine just because you have a great idea is the better option. How you choose to fund the business takes what? Planning. Exactly. Whether you get it the old traditional way through banks or self-fund the business, you have to have some cash at the end of the day.

Money or lack thereof didn't bother Reggie. By nature, he was a hustler. I saw him make things happen when it came to money. Maybe he knew of a big hole in the sky where the money came crashing down to the earth for the pickings. I'm just saying. I don't know. What I did know was that his approach was unconventional.

He often threw caution to the wind and went full speed ahead, calculating cost on any piece of paper he could find lying around the house. There were sticky notes with numbers and calculations floating around everywhere. No doubt, he was aware he would need money to get and keep the business going. However, his response to most questions regarding money was he'd get to that later. He wasn't concerned with it at all.

When it came to the business, and because he wasn't generating revenue just yet, I covered the bills and floated money to him for the business. Initially, it was a breeze, since I'd already had a cush savings from my paychecks. As I noticed expenses were starting to come up more with trucking, I knew we needed to get in front of it. He shared what he expected the expenses were going to be monthly, and after much consideration, I decided my $50k credit card would fund the business until we could turn a profit or at least until business picked up. I expressed the need to make sure that the balance stayed as minimal as possible. He agreed that I would handle the household with my check, and he would handle the credit card charges with the money he made from the business.

Looking back, I'm not sure that was the right decision to see how things ended between us. But more on that later in the story. So, Reggie used my credit cards to float the truck expenses, whether for fuel, toll charges, or lumper fees. Oh, and don't forget the maintenance for the truck and trailer. Baby, you talking about a hefty price tag. Ouch! Yep, it all went on the credit card. Every month, I saw the charges rack up. I'd remind him the bill was due and wait for him to give me the money to pay the bill. And he did. But, wait for it. It was only enough to pay the minimum payment. So, what do you think that did to the bill each month? You guessed it. The interest alone was ridiculous. No matter how much it chapped my ass, I took money from my hard-earned paycheck and paid more each month, so I could keep the balance low enough not to affect my debt ratio.

I remember a time I was planning a girl's night out to paint and sip. During the time, I kept my credit cards in a wallet in the top dresser drawer. I went to retrieve one of the cards and notice my Discover card was missing. My gut told me that he took it and was using it. I told myself I'd better brace myself for what was coming next. I went to the office where he was working and asked him if he had it. He casually looked up at me and, with a grimacing look of disgust, answered yes. I asked him what he was using it for and without my knowledge. He said he took it because he needed it. I asked if he had intended to tell me that he took the card. I met his response with disbelief. Reggie told me he didn't have to tell me anything, and since he no longer had to answer to his momma, he damn sure wasn't going to answer to me.

Geez. It was ridiculous. And, it got worse over a brief period. That's when I knew I needed God's help to keep me sane in the marriage. I was losing a battle I didn't sign up to fight, and only He could help me see the truth of it all.

Fighting for his Attention

"Hey. Hey, you (tap...tap...tap). Hey, I know you see me over here. Excuse me, can't you hear me calling yo' name? Hellloooo. Urrrgh! You get on my damn nerves ignoring me... I know you didn't look at me like that. You might want to say something; then you wouldn't need to look at me cockeyed. You must be out of yo' damn mind. Now I forgot what I was calling you about."

Does that sound familiar to anybody out there? How annoying is it to feel you're being ignored? You know for certain, and I mean for damn certain, they can hear you and see you 'cause you're right in their face. But no...they continue doing what they were doing and never acknowledge or even answer you. You can go so far as to pound your fist on the table. No matter how much you scream or play mind games just to get their attention, nothing seems to work. Have you ever been there? Ever felt like that? Well, I sure have. I felt like that with Reggie. Ha! I'm mad all over again typing it—damn flashbacks.

Okay, where was I? Oh yeah, Reggie worked nonstop, over the road, late nights, early mornings, including in his sleep. No. I'm serious. He would sometimes talk in his sleep or mumble something about trucking. Good got-damnit! I couldn't escape trucking. I had to deal with it during the day (yes, while I was at work), when we were home in the evenings, and now in his sleep. WTF.

Somehow, I became his secretary. He called me at work and asked me to fax documents to suppliers. He called to ask me to pay lumper fees. He'd called me to complete his carrier packets because he was driving, and it had to be immediate.

It became an ongoing thing. Mind you, I had work from my job to finish, and now I played a secretary for the business. Therefore, my work split between his business and my career.

When I came home from work, there Reggie was at the computer. When I walked over to him and kiss him, I'd ask how his day went. Immediately, he started with truck talk. He'd go on and on and never realized he didn't stop to ask me how my day had gone. It wasn't fair, but I understood, I guess. The business was his thing, and I needed to get that through my thick skull sooner rather than later.

There were times when he came up for air, and it was a pleasant surprise to see him away from the computer. But even with that, I noticed our discussions were mostly about the business, if not all. Every waking moment, the business occupied his time, space, and energy. Very little time was for me, and it took its toll on me. I wanted him to talk to me about me or at least about us. I wanted to have a stupid crazy laugh with him from time to time. I needed to get some alone time regularly, and that wasn't too much to ask. I wanted us to go back to a few weeks earlier when our love was thick and it swallowed me up. So, there was only one thing for me to do, addressed it. But how? How could I express my feelings without him thinking I was ungrateful? I certainly didn't want to come across as being "that" chick who begged continuously for her husband's attention. By no means was I going to resort to being the wife who "nagged" her husband for every little thing. I wasn't about to become that dripping faucet the Bible speaks of in Proverbs 27:15. Nope, But I had to say or do something.

I decided to soften the approach by asking Reggie how the business was going. I expressed to him how proud I was of him for even taking on the challenge of going into business. I asked if he needed anything from me to make things easier. He told me there wasn't anything he needed; he just needed to stay focused. Crap! He wanted to stay focused, and I wanted to distract him. Can you say a dilemma? Oh well, I went for it. I had to get my time in one way or the other.

I jumped right in feet first and asked Reggie when he would spend time with me. He said we would have plenty of time when the business was where he needed it to be. He went on to say it was for his family and reminded me of what he said before, “When I lock in on something, I won’t let it go, and that’s where I am right now. I have to get this business running successfully.”

There I stood, feeling somewhat defeated because although I understood how important the business was for him, I felt I was no longer a priority. It was as if I were an outsider looking into his newfound lease on life and the business venture, longing to be a part of it with him but unable to. I didn’t know how to break through to get his attention, at least not anymore. It was apparent that our marriage suffered because Reggie’s time and attention were solely on the business. I’d fought for his attention before with golf. And once again, I’m fighting for his attention with the business. A sister can’t win for losing.

As time went on, more and more, I migrated into the background. It was becoming very apparent that golf and business were eclipsing our marriage by then. I increasingly became more frustrated at the whole damn thing.

I tried to be patient and continued to encourage Reggie to make time for us. Look, it’s no easy task for a wife to compete with anything in her marriage. And it’s equally disheartening, knowing I was competing for his attention with golf and business of all things. As he focused on the business during the week, I planned time for us on the weekend. I often planned for us to do something together on the days he wasn’t working, only to find out that he’d made plans to go golfing with his buddies. It didn’t take an ounce of brainpower for him to jump all over the opportunity when his golf buddies called on the weekend or whenever he wasn't working. He rushed out to the golf course with them without hesitation, even when he knew beforehand that I had planned something for us to do.

I admit I was pissed about all of it. I questioned Reggie's love for me. Yep, six months into the marriage, he no longer had time for me. He lost sight that he had a wife who needed him as well. On multiple occasions, I heard that I had to wait for his attention to hang out together; he would tell me to wait until things were where they needed to be, then he would have all the time in the world for me. And just like that, just like a hurt little girl, I would retreat. What more could I do?

CHAPTER FOUR

He Changed Hands

A Change Is Coming

One of the most hurtful things I've had to experience in a relationship is feeling dismissed or blown off. It made me feel that what I was saying (or feeling) didn't matter or wasn't significant. For instance, someone may minimize what you've said or your opinion and make it trivial and not worth listening to. Or, they might take it, turn it around, or twist it to fit their agenda in full disregard of what you said. By the way, that's called gaslighting.

Throughout my marriage, Reggie continually dismissed me. He said anything he wanted and didn't care how it made me feel. When we talked about our marriage, Reggie would sit most times with a blank look on his face, with no response. He'd blow up so quickly to leave and end the discussion, leaving me feeling dismissed.

After a while, things began to change drastically. It wasn't comfortable talking to my husband, and I found myself shutting down and giving up. And what good would it be to keep hitting my head against a brick wall or, in this case, a brick heart? I retreated and did the only thing I felt was left for me to do: get my feelings out by journaling. I recall one day he and I had a massive blow-up. I remember sitting on the guest bed upstairs with tears rolling down my face. I picked up my journal and started writing all the horrible things my husband said to me until that point in 2016 (yep, a year into the marriage). I must warn you that what I'm about to share is unfathomable. No wife, woman, or girlfriend should hear the things I did coming from a man's mouth, let alone my husband. Remember, Matthew 12:34b says, "For the mouth speaks what the heart is full of ," and some pretty vile things in Reggie's heart spewed out of his mouth toward me.

Put Ya' Mouth on Me

My husband wasn't a confrontational person when we first met. However, over time, and a short period at that, he became verbally abusive. He didn't yell, fuss, or fight, but his words cut deeply. I'm convinced that he didn't want to be bothered by my constant discussions about the marriage because he engrossed himself in business. Reggie couldn't think about anything else, and when I came at him, he said the most hurtful things to make me go away.

I began journaling what I went through, and that included the words he said to me. Without batting an eye, Reggie said these exact words to me.

"You talk too much; why don't you shut up sometimes?"

"You're too needy, and I don't have time for you. I'll do it when I feel like it."

"You always got to have a plan for something. Quit overthinking shit so much and just go with what I said."

"You fucking nag too much. Why can't you leave shit alone?"

"Don't ask me about going to church no more; I said I ain't

going. I was vetting you to see if you were a Christian woman because I wanted to see if you could get a prayer through."

"I don't have to apologize to you. I ain't sorry."

"No, I don't love you. I don't want to be with you anymore."

"I could have paid my truck off if I wasn't here paying bills."

The sad part about it is that he didn't see anything wrong with any of the things he said.

Okay, okay. Close ya' mouth. I know, right.

But here's the kicker, after a year or so of marriage, the intimacy between us stopped. Yep, ya' heard me right. Even with that, I was still trying to get his attention by throwing the panties at him for sex, until one fateful day when he told me to quit asking him for sex, and then he said, "I don't want to screw you, so you can fuck anybody you want. I don't care."

Now, there's no doubt there was some truth to the things he said. Yes, I talk a lot (I know how to communicate). I can't just leave shit alone (I like to resolve issues). Yes, we all know I have to have a plan (I said that from the beginning). Yes, I asked him to do things around the house as any wife would. Again, there's some truth to these things. But no way in hell did he have to say the things he did. I didn't make him say those things because of my actions. No, he chose to say them to piss me off and make me shut down, go away, or, perhaps, even divorce. His words hurt. It took a lot for me to stay and keep my vows. Sure, this seems a bit much, mainly because I didn't put the full context around it. But, if I were to do that, this book would be 800 baskillion pages long.

Fast forward a couple of weeks after I journaled his comments. Reggie and I were sitting in the garage one Saturday morning drinking coffee and smoking a cigarette. I mentioned to him I had been thinking about all the inconsiderate and vile things he's ever said to me and how he'd never apologized for them. He had the nerve to ask me for examples. I was happy to oblige and gave him a few of his choice words to me. Initially, he laughed under his breath and denied ever saying any of it. I had to prove my point to him, so I excused myself and went to get the journal. I handed him the journal, and as he flipped through the pages, his facial expression almost (I said almost) showed shame or embarrassment. He did his best to keep a straight face, but his eyes revealed the truth as he read his disturbing words. When he finished reading, he turned his back and looked out of the garage. I asked, "Is this bringing back any memories?" He paused briefly and said, "Yeah, I guess I did, huh."

That's it. Even after Reggie's acknowledgment, I still didn't get an apology. That moment showed me I was fighting a battle I wouldn't win. All I wanted was for him to get a glimpse of how much pain he'd caused me and apologize. But pride wouldn't let him. And this, my friends, is the man I married! No, I'm sorry; he was the man who showed up after we married.

Eyes Wide Shut

Reggie failed to realize he woke up the sleeping bear, and she was coming for him. At times, I was so angry and despised him for taking me through unnecessary bullshit. I wanted badly to show him the old St. Louis chick who lay dormant and give back to him every ounce of vileness he gave to me. I tried every day not to be that woman. I knew it wouldn't be right, so I chose to refrain. But I'd be lying if I said I didn't want to cuss him out. Deep in my heart, I wanted to hurt him because he hurt me. Each time I looked at Reggie, my stomach turned. I finally saw who and what he was. I had to face the fact that I chose him to be my husband for the rest of my life.

All I could ask myself was why. Why put up with the bull? Talk about kicking yourself in the butt. I beat myself up for being so stupid and dreaded answering the questions that were swimming around in my head. I beat myself up for allowing Reggie to dismiss me, for staying with him, knowing he didn't love me or perhaps hated the very ground I walked on.

I know I took more than enough crap from my husband than I would from anyone else. I questioned if I'd ever reach my breaking point. With enough to sort through, I had much soul-searching to do. Quite frankly, either I was in denial or a plum fool because there was no way Reggie could mean that much to me with how he treated me. This disrespectful behavior certainly wasn't what I had in mind for marriage with him. No freaking way. Nope. Nadda.

The more I sat in my truth, the more pissed I became. I would go so far to admit I had a little bit of hatred in my heart toward Reggie. I released all my feelings on paper when he didn't apologize after reading the horrible things he said to me. I called out everything I'd held in before. Everything I couldn't say before, I let flow. I journaled that he was irresponsible and didn't take accountability for his actions. Reggie was a manipulator, disrespectful, and rude. He couldn't hold an intelligent conversation. He didn't act like a man with a wife, didn't lead his household, and only thought of himself. He lied to and used others for his benefit. He was inconsiderate, pretended to be someone he wasn't, and made excuses for everything regarding our marriage. Reggie convinced others he was a "good" person, but he twisted the truth to keep it from coming back on him. Whew. Yep, that's how I started to see Reggie, and I was mad as hell about the whole thing.

Reggie took from my life and added nothing. Deciding if I should walk away from my marriage weighed on my heart. I had mixed emotions because I made a vow. However, I had to look at the situation and decide if I loved him or if I loved the idea of being married. OUCH. Was I willing to sacrifice my happiness, self-worth, and sanity for the sake of staying married? However, those questions paled in comparison to my thoughts of God's view of my marriage state. Urgh. It was just too much, too soon, and for no damn good reason.

Considering all that I had endured the first 18 months of marriage, I convinced myself that Reggie was hiding something. He was in complete denial, thinking that this marriage and its issues were 100% my fault. But it wasn't about pointing fingers. It was about being accountable for ourselves in the marriage. We should have asked what we could do differently to make the marriage better. I did my assessments of what I wanted to do differently, but when I brought it to him to talk about it, he dismissed me. It takes two people to hold a marriage together. But one person can bring it to ruins.

Don't Change a Good Thing (GT)

Looking back at my marriage, it was nothing I expected. In the newlywed marriage stage, we had a new business that Reggie was married to instead of me. His extra-curricular activity of golf was his girlfriend, and I was slowly fading into the background. Well, honestly, I was no longer in the picture period.

My marriage's staleness was new to me and left my heart fragile and desperately wanting his attention. I made myself available to him when he wanted to talk "shop" about the business. Even when I couldn't care less about it, I still showed him I supported him. I invested time and energy into him despite how he mistreated me; I still wanted to be the GT (a good thing) I vowed to be.

I didn't want his behavior to cause me to react in an unloving way, especially if I genuinely wanted my marriage to resemble a loving and devoted one. He was unwilling to recognize the severity of our marriage problems or lack of commitment to me. I couldn't retaliate by going off, cursing him out, and disrespecting him because it would make things between us worse. So, I chose to love him through it all, even if it hurt.

As time continued, he pulled himself further away from me. Although we weren't arguing, we weren't speaking to each other, unless it was about the business, the house, or bills. That's it—nothing more and nothing less. We had a few laughs here and there, but everything was surface. There was no depth or connection to how we interacted with each other. I walked around on eggshells so I wouldn't piss him off or push him out of the door. I second-guessed asking simple questions because I didn't want to argue.

My choice of not expressing myself was probably not the best way to handle the situation. It did me no good and ultimately pushed me further into the outskirts of our marriage. That was better than hearing him disrespect me. Instead, I let things be with him and figured it out on my own.

I couldn't bear the hurt, knowing he no longer saw me. That's when I made a conscious decision to take charge of my marriage and do what I could do to bring unity back into a place of division and peace back into a place of strife. I had to do something to feel good about myself and my marriage. I brought my Bible and books on marriage to read and created for myself a safe space, my war room. This was going to be the space for reflection on me, my husband, and our marriage. I had to get a plan together on how to save our marriage, or else Reggie and I would end up divorced, which wasn't an option, at least for me.

About Us

There were rumblings in late 2017 that there would be a reduction in force (RIF) in our HR department, which presented an opportunity for me to leave the corporate world and step out as an entrepreneur and help my husband with the trucking business. I will admit this was very exciting to me. Reggie would often comment on my work and encourage me to open my own consulting company. It was something I'd thought of before but never pursued. I had been seriously considering the idea of starting a business and mentioned it to him. He was all for the idea and said he thought I would be great at having my own business. We also talked about expanding the trucking business into freight brokering, which made sense since it was in full force. So, we moved forward with the idea.

January 2018, we finally got the word that a reduction in force (RIF) was going to occur, the number of people affected, and the option to "voluntarily" leave the company. I thought this was the perfect time to exit on my terms and support him. After receiving all the information and immediately arriving home, I called a family meeting with him and my youngest son. I wanted to share the information and get their input. After giving them all the details, Reggie said I should have done what he called "invest in yourself" earlier, and I had his full support. We discussed the bills, and he said he wasn't worried about the bills because he had that covered. So, I made the decision. All agreed. I went back to work and submitted my notice to leave the company voluntarily after 19 years. And so, I did. My future was in the hands of my supportive husband. At least, I thought it was.

Part of my leaving AT&T came with a hefty sum of money. Money has always been an issue with him and me from the start, but by this time, we were in the right place financially. It was good that we were no longer arguing about money, since he'd landed a nice contract connected to Walmart. I started planning how we would use the severance pay and considered which bills to pay off first.

Now, I was the money handler in the marriage. I had spreadsheets to track expenses and budgeted everything we had. Look, I'm a planner by nature; it's in my DNA. And I document everything that relates to finances. I never worried about money. I had money and managed it well, and Reggie knew it. When the time came to discuss what I had planned for the money, I knew he would be okay with whatever I outlined.

One night, sitting up in the bed talking, he asked what I would do with the money. I told him I would pay off a few bills and leave the rest for both of our business expenses. He nodded his head in agreement but never mentioned anything specifically about the trucking business. I assured him I would give him the list once finished, and the numbers were together. The day finally came after I left the company when I reviewed everything with him, line by line. I asked if we were good to move forward, to which he said yes. But I noticed he was hesitant afterward, and I couldn't put my finger on it.

Nonetheless, we agreed that we would use the money to pay off individual bills and still had money left over to invest in my new business and support his. I left my job in February 2018, and it felt invigorating. I was ready to take on business with my husband and start my consulting firm, hoping this would get us back on track in our marriage.

Did You Say No Support?

Immediately after leaving AT&T, I felt an excitement I hadn't felt in years. I would be working with my husband and venturing out to build my own business. Despite it being much work, I was helping him with the business, and one thing I knew was all things HR; so, I could handle it. However, as days and weeks passed by, he became more and more silent. I mean, now and then, he would throw a suggestion out but never really into helping me. He no longer offered ideas. Even when I asked about the brokerage's next steps, he would give me that old "nothing right now; I'll let you know." I couldn't understand it because we paid the broker's bond, so I didn't understand what the holdup was all about. Something was bothering him, but he wasn't sharing his concerns with me. So, I moved forward and focused on getting the business set up.

Within a month after my exit, I paid all the bills and established my business, we had a very nice contract with Wal-Mart, and life seemed steady again. There wasn't anything to argue about. All should have been good, right? Well, it wasn't.

I felt a shift in the atmosphere, and let me tell you, it was dark energy all around. Reggie had a relentless funk about him. So, what did I do? I asked him what in the hell was wrong with him because I couldn't take it anymore, and his response chopped me in the throat. "You don't support me, and you don't believe in the vision. You knew I've been saying we needed to buy another truck, and you took that money from AT&T and paid your bills off. You didn't give me anything, and now I'm stuck paying all the bills. Now you got your business..."

He continued with his rant, but by that time, I didn't hear anything. I'm telling you, my mouth hit the floor and bounced off four walls. I couldn't believe this shit. I had completely blocked him out with all the thoughts that raced through my mind. All I could think was, *Are we getting ready to do this again, right now? Now that I've walked away from my job, you want to pick a fucking fight on some bullshit?* That old list was coming back to mind, and no, I wasn't thinking about speaking life over him, not while he was trying to kill my moment.

At that moment, every thought of not only how I supported him to get the trucking business off the ground but every negative thing that he'd ever said or done to me came rushing to my mind. Looking at him with disdain; I thought to myself, *No support? Not only did I support you, but I carried yo' ass from jump street. I put up with your bullshitting lackadaisical ass ways. I overlooked your funky ass disposition in this marriage. I offered to help you get the truck, and you ran to yo' momma because I couldn't pull the money out of MY 401K (oh, 'cause you don't have one...uh-huh). Still, I was the one who put the equipment on MY credit card (since yo' dumb ass ran yours into the ground) so you could get your business. Huh? I was the one who paid all the bills out of my check every month while you piecemealed me a little money here and a little money there. But I was cool with that because I supported yo' ass. Ohh, I was the one who gave you MY $50K credit card while you were over the road, and yo' ass got swipe-happy with my shit. You disrespectful, ungrateful, inconsiderate, half-ass mother&*%. Who was the one who paid the credit card bills every month? Uh-huh, that would be ME. WHAT. Are you kidding me? Get the f&*% outta here with that bull.*

Every bit of that went spiraling through my mind. My thoughts continued to run ramped as I glared at him. *You throw a tantrum about the money I received from working hard for 19 years. Oh, now it's about us? It wasn't about us before when I asked yo ass to spend time with me, and all you wanted to do was work and golf. But now you mad about my money, and PRIDE kept you from saying something when I asked you a month ago about what we should do for the household. You're an idiot. So you're mad? Well, stay mad!*

Whew! I held a lot inside. Out of touch for a few seconds, it felt good to unleash it in my head. If only I said it aloud. Instead, I stood there, glaring at Reggie as he glared at me. I didn't realize that I had reached the tipping point in my mind. Nor had I realize how pissed he was at me because I hadn't given him any of my surplus money. I asked him what he was talking about because we had money in the bank. He said, "Well, you didn't give it to me; it's in your bank. It's funny how you let the White man (Edwards Jones) manage your money, but you can't invest in your husband." Then he walked off.

WOW! I couldn't believe what I'd just heard. The thought of him making the moment I was most excited all about him messed me up. I knew for sure he was a crazy-ass con man with bipolar tendencies. I shrugged it and him off and went back to what I was doing, and you know where he went, right? Yep, golfing. That's when everything went downhill fast.

CHAPTER FIVE

Her Praying Hands

Talk about being on edge. I had just left my job, and Reggie and I were barely speaking since the blow-up about the money. But, can I be honest? I didn't want my marriage to end. I figured the pressure of running the business and marriage took a toll on him. I felt empathy for him. I realized that if I wanted to see a change in my marriage, I had to be the one to change—big ol' me. If Reggie couldn't do it, then I needed to stand in the gap for him. Hell, I did everything else, so this shouldn't be a big deal, right.

Flip the Script

I was determined to speak life my dead situation. I was reminded of the Bible story of the valley of dry bones one day as I thought about my marriage. In the story, God had asked Ezekiel if the bones could live, and he responded by saying, "Only you know that God." Only God knew if my marriage would live again, so I had to inquire of Him to change how I thought about it. So, I made a personal request and asked God to change my heart. I asked him to show me myself, mostly my heart, and what He wanted me to get out of the situation. I didn't want a divorce despite the horrible way he mistreated me. Call me crazy, but you won't call me a quitter, especially when I knew what God could do for me.

I flipped all the negative thoughts and words I spoke about Reggie with positive words. I had to undo everything negative thing I'd said, ask for forgiveness, and speak positivity. I changed what I spoke angrily to a blessing over him and I, of course, tried my best to see the good in him.

I knew I couldn't stop there, so my prayers shifted from Reggie to God and me. I asked God to reveal my motives and expose what was deep in my heart that kept me in this place of darkness. It couldn't only be about my husband. I was sure I had some "issues" myself. I wanted no stone left unturned on this one. I was determined to fall back and watch God do his thing. I knew that the power of life and death was in my mouth (Prov 18:21), and I would have what I say if I didn't doubt (Matt 21:21).

I knew my marriage was under attack. We both were. God's said to Eve, "Your desire will be for your husband" (Gen 3:16). The enemy knows that if he can place a wedge between husband and wife, they'll fight against one another until death comes to the marriage. Don't get it twisted, "till death do us part" doesn't solely mean physical death. It can be any death within marriage, such as the death of love, fidelity, respect, unity, finances, and more. I'm sure you get the picture. Mark 3:25 says, "if a house divides against itself, that house cannot stand." That's what happened in my marriage, and I saw it coming. He wasn't attending church any longer. He didn't pray for or with me. I never saw him open a Bible or read it for that matter. The door was wide open for the enemy to attack my household's head because there was no protection around it.

Neither of us was perfect in the marriage, and that wasn't the expectation. But God was. I knew God could change me while I was waiting on Him to change my husband. God would give me the strength to endure it all. With all the hurt, heartbreak, and disappointment I'd already suffered, everything else to come would be a cakewalk. So, it was time to go to war with words.

Stay and Pray

During this fragile time, I prayed all the more for him and our marriage. But it seemed the more I prayed, the worse things became. After a while, I'd started sleeping upstairs and away from our bed. I couldn't stand to look at him anymore. He didn't care one way or the other, and I needed to figure out what my next steps would be. We didn't talk to each other much, and the numbness had settled in between us. I was starting to realize that I didn't want to do this marriage thing anymore; moreover, I didn't have to if this was the way it was always going to be.

Anytime a wife leaves the marriage bed, and the husband makes no attempts to find out what's going on, ask questions, show empathy, or anything, guess what? He no longer cares. That's what my husband demonstrated to me. I saw in his eyes that I no longer added value to him.

So, what was I to do? My problem was trying to discover which decision would please God. I didn't take the situation lightly because everything was at stake. I had to consider how I would move forward and put myself first, since my husband wouldn't.

Whenever I thought I had reached the point of walking away, the thought of my vows to him and God crossed my mind. I felt in my spirit, God reminding me that I'd asked Him for help, but I hadn't given it all to Him. I asked God to show me what it all meant, so I had to trust Him.

I didn't believe that God would allow me to go through all this emotional and mental turmoil without getting the lesson. And believe me, I wanted to know what it all meant because I wanted out of this twilight zone. The relationship with Reggie flipped off like a light switch. It consumed me, and I lost myself in the process. The woman I became was unrecognizable.

At the Hands of HIM

CHAPTER SIX

Living in Confusion

Your eyes will see strange sights, and your mind will imagine confusing things. ~ *Proverbs 23:33 (NIV)*

Imagine driving on the road in your car with your window down. The sun is shining, and you feel the breeze blowing against your face. The music's playing, and as you vibe to the sounds coming from the radio, your mind wanders off, and all is peaceful. Suddenly, out of nowhere, you notice the sky ahead with storm clouds forming. Although a little concerned, you're not worried because the weather didn't call for storms. As you continue ahead, you notice the clouds are getting thicker, and the sky turns dark gray. The wind starts to pick up and is now blowing with a mighty force. Raindrops begin to hit the windshield as if you drove into a waterfall. Your nerves kick in as you weren't expecting a storm to accompany the trip.

You see something ahead that looks like a tunnel. Your fingers tightly grip the steering wheel at ten and two. You straighten up in the seat to focus clearly. As you approach the opening of the tunnel, you hear a weird sound coming from your engine. You think to yourself, *No way, this is a brand-new car.* The engine starts to rattle and shake uncontrollably. Your heart beats fast as the car spits and stutters. Looking around, you wonder what the heck is going on because all hell is breaking loose.

You're in the middle of a storm, and the one thing protecting you is on the verge of breaking down; your car.

The car creeps toward the tunnel's opening; as a clash of lightning strikes in front of the car, you belt out a scream. Your only hope is to make it into the tunnel. The car pulls forward. Darkness from the sky and tunnel surrounds you. You're in total disbelief of how the storm came out of nowhere. Thinking of what to do next, the car engine suddenly dies.

In the middle of nowhere, surrounded by darkness, you feel your breath getting short. You can barely swallow due to the massive lump in your throat, your stomach begins to ache, and fear comes over you like a rushing flood. But you noticed the wind is no longer blowing. The calming of the storm is good because at least you can think now.

"Think, think," you say out loud. After taking a deep breath, you go through a mental checklist for the car. "I have air in the tires, the battery is all right (or at least it was), I have gas in the car, I hadn't had any problems since I bought the car. So, what's going on?" you yell.

Suddenly, you have an ah-ha moment. You reach for your cell phone, and much to your surprise, the battery level is 25%, but it has zero bars. "Crap! No reception. Great, just great," you say in disgust. Things just took a turn for the worse. As you sit, thoughts of what if, fear, death, and loneliness surface. You're racing to come up with something, anything to get you out of there. You realized you're all alone. You slump down in the seat with your head in your hands and sob uncontrollably. You pray for God to help you. The more you pray, the more fear grips you. You shout, "God, are you listening to me? Where are you, and why did you leave me out here?

Moments pass, and you say, "Manual." Yes, the manual. There has to be something in there that will help fix this mess." Leaning forward to open the glove compartment, you grab the manual. You reach for your key chain for the small key light. Breathing a sigh of relief, you ask, "Now, where do I start?" You tell yourself you better start at the beginning because you have no idea where the breakdown came from, internally or externally. But you have a good idea that it came from both.

After what seemed an eternity, you look up and realize some time has passed. Looking straight ahead, you can tell the clouds are moving away. A sliver of light starts to peek through the tunnel ahead. You jump at the idea to position the key fob directly on the push-to-start button to recharge the system. The car sputters, and the lights on the dashboard flicker. You begin to get hopeful that you'll get out of the tunnel soon.

Sitting back, you take a deep breath. You try the key again. This time, the car turns over, and the engine begins to roar. Your body stiffens in the seat as you think not to jinx anything. You tell yourself to calm down and relax. As you wiggle forward in the seat, you put the gear in drive, and the car begins to move forward but slowly. "Careful," you tell yourself as you remember what just happened. Nevertheless, you give the car a little more gas, and it starts on a steady roll. Feeling a bit more confident as you move forward, the car sputters and shuts down.

"No, no, no, not again," you whisper; your heart sinks, and fear grips your soul. Determined not to give up, you place the car in park and thumb through the manual to review what you learned. You keep your eyes forward on the beam of light shining ahead at the end of the tunnel. You tell yourself, "All right, so much has happened, but I've got what I need right in my hands. I have to remember what I've learned. If I do what the book says, I'll live to tell the story."

Taking a deep breath in, you started the engine again, and, this time, you give it a little more gas. You're now moving forward with both hands on the wheel. You give it more gas. You begin rolling steadily toward the light. You see the light at the end of the tunnel. A smile starts to form on your face. The landscaping starts to appear ahead. You're getting closer to the other side of the tunnel. All you have to do is keep going, keep moving, keep looking forward. That's what you tell yourself as the car begins to pick up speed. As you approached the tunnel's opening on the other side, your heart beats with excitement because you can see again. Yes, the darkness has lifted. The moments of doom and gloom are no longer a threat.

Life ahead is exhilarating, and you aren't going to stop. The moment you break through the tunnel's end, you can feel the light's warmth beat through the windshield as it surrounds the car. It's clear, bright, and peaceful. Full speed ahead, you glance in the rearview mirror. You smile with a tear rolling down your cheek as you watch the tunnel fading away. "Yes, I made it to the other side," you yell with your head out the window.

Sitting tall in the seat and with your "manual" in your lap, you say with confidence, "Let's go. I'm ready to get to where I'm supposed to be now."

Let's Press Rewind

Very early in the morning of September 17, 2018, I was lying on my bed, eyes wide open, staring at the wall. I had never felt this numb before in life. Oddly enough, I hadn't slept in "our" bed with Reggie for months, and now he was gone. I mean gone… gone. I couldn't tell if I was breathing or if it was all a dream because everything was unrecognizable to me. Come to think of it, I don't even think my eyes blinked while I was lying there. All I felt was an emptiness so thick and heavy because I was in complete shock. I just couldn't believe it. What the hell just happened last night? The police? Really? We've had arguments about bills before, but this one, this one was different. I kept thinking about how we ended up in this jacked up situation. Flashes of the night before rushed in again. I could still see the look in his eyes, eyes that were dark and full of evil. I didn't even recognize him as my husband. He was a stranger.

I replayed Reggie sitting in the garage taunting me as he said, "Oh, I ain't broke you yet? You're so damn stupid. Why do you want to be with a man that doesn't fucking love you? I'm going to break you if it's the last thing I do."

"Why. Why do you want to break your wife?" I asked.

"Because you ain't shit. You wouldn't give me the money when I needed it the most, and now you want me to pay some fucking bills."

Just like that, everything went blank. I stood up and walked toward Reggie as the rage boiled within me. I pushed him as hard as I could. He looked at me with a slight grin on his face and said, "Push me again and see what happens. Put your hands on me again, and I'm calling the police."

Yeah, right, I thought to myself. He wouldn't dare call the police on his wife. Before he could finish the sentence, I pushed him again. He jumped to his feet, phone in hand, and dialed 9-1-1. He walked back into the house toward the bedroom as I heard him speaking with the operator on the other end of the phone. He turned and looked at me with so much hatred in his eyes and said, "When I get through telling them you threatened me and put your hands on me, they'll be telling you to leave this house. I stood there in unbelief. The only thing I could say to him was, "Really, the police? You going to call the police on your wife?"

"You' damn right," he said.

I realized in my visitations to the past that he did the same thing by calling the police on me when we were dating. As I stated before, when I called the police, he lied about what took place, and there he was again blowing things out of proportion. Talk about life coming back full circle. He didn't care about me then, and some five years later, he still didn't. At least he was consistent in his behavior. Pretty much the way he came into the relationship with his explosive behavior was the same way he went out of the marriage. A leopard never changes its spots.

While he was speaking with the operator, I grabbed my phone and called his mother. If anyone was able to talk him down, it was her. I placed her on speaker, and she heard him reporting me. She yelled, "You don't call the police on your wife; what in the hell is wrong with you?" He didn't care. He was insistent on conjuring up his story to report me. This incident was the ticket he needed to start his escape plan to leave me and the marriage.

Shortly before the police arrived, I called my sons to have them come to the house. I didn't know what was about to happen, but I knew it wouldn't end well. The officers spoke with us separately. As things would turn out, they didn't believe his story enough to feel I was the threat, so they made him leave the house. They asked him to grab a few things quickly and leave. As we waited for him to get his belongings, he took longer than expected, so they kept asking him just to grab a few things and leave. It seemed like an eternity as I watched him gather his belongings. Reggie packed everything he could load into his car. That's when it hit me; he's not coming back.

After my husband left, my world turned upside down. I felt like I was suffocating like something was trying to kill me. Deep in depression, all I could do was relive the moment he left. I replayed it over and over again until I felt empty and alone. As that cycle continued, I believed anything that would help it all make sense. I'm not sure if I made it up or if the darkness led me to believe lies about myself, my marriage, and my husband. They had to be from the enemy because of the darkness that surrounded me. The longer I focused on the lies, the tighter the chokehold was around my neck as I fought through the aftermath of Reggie walking.

Hello Darkness

The weight of what happened hit me like a bulldozer, but I mustered up enough strength to sit up in the bed as I looked around the room. Everything seemed eerie because Reggie was no longer there. I was hurt, you know, but, mostly, I was confused. I didn't know what to do, and I surely couldn't call him. That wouldn't be good.

My throat began to dry up as the tears started to flow. I could still see Reggie's face, empty and sinister. Everything we went through as husband and wife flashed right before my eyes: the good, the bad, the ugly, and now this, the worst. What may have been a few seconds seemed as if it were hours as I tried to shake the thoughts loose in my head. The darkness was closing in on me, as if it were saying, "Hello. I've been waiting for you for quite some time now. May I sit down?" Without a second to think, just like that (snap of a finger), I welcomed in the darkness like a broken little girl all alone.

I replayed the incident in my head at least a million times. Then reality choked the life out of me. He's truly gone this time. It was the eleventh time my husband left. Yes. You heard me correctly: eleven. As I lay there, so many questions flooded my mind. "Now what? What are you going to do without any money? How are you going to pay the mortgage? Worse yet, the bills? How could you not see this coming? Why in the hell did you walk away from your job? Are you freaking crazy, girl? What the hell is wrong with you?" Sadly enough, I never thought I would ever have to answer these kinds of questions. Humph, I guess I had that one all the way wrong.

Have you ever been in such a dark place that no matter how strong you knew you were, you couldn't do anything? What about that good ol' Bible verse that says, "I can do all this through him (Christ) who gives me strength" (Philippians 4:13)? Well, I knew one thing, it was going to have to be Christ because I was a weak wreck. No one, especially me, expects to go through this kind of betrayal. Most times, we go through the day without taking inventory of the reality right in front of our faces. We expect things to be the same because that's how things have been. Ah, but that's when we get thrown for a loop. Not to mention all the sense our momma gave us goes right out the door. We end up broken in our hearts, our lives, and our minds. Yep, that was me. I was betrayed and broken.

Although I was living my worst nightmare, I needed to do something. After all, when Reggie calmed down, he'd come back, and we would work through our marriage. I couldn't let this blow-up stop me. Get a "plan" is what I told myself (there I go again with my plans). I had no doubt he'd come back after a few days, so I needed to prepare to go all in for my marriage, so I would be ready when he walked through the door. I needed something to believe in at the time, so I talked myself into preparing for him to come back. I grabbed my journal, pens, highlighters, and my Bible. (Silence). Okay, girl, what ya' going to do now, huh? It hit me hard.

My mind raced back to him. I couldn't do anything but cry. Yep, that's what I did. I cried day after day and night after night for the first week after he left. By then, it was apparent he wasn't coming back as I'd hoped. The dread of it all threw me deeper into depression. I cried out to God and begged Him to help me. I felt the pains in my heart. It was breaking into pieces as I thought of him and the fun times we had. I dared not think about the bad stuff (yet) even though I was hurting deeply because of him walking out. Correction, not just him walking out, but all the things he did while he was there. But I would take that all back if it would stop the pain in my heart. I couldn't understand how one person could cause that much pain to another. It was far beyond my understanding. I couldn't eat or sleep for continually thinking about it all. It was, indeed, challenging to focus on my businesses. All I could do was cry and ask God to help me.

As time passed, the more depressed I became. I was alone in the house we once lived in together. I remember feeling embarrassed at what happened. Why did I feel embarrassed? He was the one who did this to us, not me. It didn't matter because it only meant I failed in my marriage, and I didn't want anyone to see me as a failure. I especially didn't want people to think I was weak, stupid, and all the rest of the things we think others will say about us. I didn't tell anyone what happened for weeks except for my kids and my best friend. I just didn't want to hear the commentary. It was bad enough I had to deal with him leaving, and the thought of having to explain something I didn't understand myself would have been worse. So, I left well enough alone and dealt with it all myself.

The reality of the bills, the mortgage, no money, loneliness, frustration, confusion, and anything else I could throw into the basket, was a heavy cloak on my back. I depressed myself into sickness. Did you hear me? I was so depressed that I got sick. Nausea and headaches were the results of crying so much and, of course, thinking negative thoughts. The deeper I sank into depression, the more I began to panic and question myself. "Why wasn't I good enough for him?" Why didn't he fight for us? What did I do to make him walk away"? I even thought, if only I had fought harder, things would have been different. But would he be different? The questions were swirling around my mind like a tornado. But they didn't change the fact he was gone.

One question after another only left me feeling worse. Somehow, I turned everything around on me and presumed I was the problem. I shouldn't have been so passive and let Reggie get away with so much. I should have stood my ground and demanded he treat me with more respect. I felt isolated, and beating up on myself didn't do much but make things worse.

So, I turned it on him. I told myself his actions up to him walking out were "part of his plan." Despite everything I did to help him achieve his goals, I convinced myself he had no intention of staying in the marriage. He planned to "level up" and used me to get there. I was a mere means to an end. And he was the one who would get to decide when it ended. I realized my end had finally come and left with no hand to hold.

So, what was I to do? I wasn't sure, but something had to happen.

CHAPTER SEVEN

Looking for God's Hand

"Come near to God and he will come near to you".
James 4:8 (NIV)

Be Still

Living in my "new normal" of abandonment and betrayal, I desperately needed to make sense out of it all. When my husband walked out, he turned my world upside down, and the only thing I could do was pray. No, cry out to God for answers, for help, for anything! I knew if anyone could help, it was Him. God knew my heart broke when Reggie left, and the pain was too much for me to handle. He was the only hope I had left.

One evening, lying in bed crying, my thoughts were all over the place. I wanted my husband back, and I didn't care what it would take for that to happen. As the tears started falling down my face, I began praying to God. I asked Him to restore my marriage. I reminded Him of the vows I had taken when I got married and begged Him to help make this right. I pointed my finger at God and demanded that He do something. I mean, since He was God, He could fix this quickly, and with a snap of His mighty finger, things would go back to the way they were before my husband left.

Thoughts swirled around in my mind like a mini tornado. In all the commotion, I heard a whisper of "Be still." At first, it caught me off guard because I would have given anything for some stillness. Laying there, I heard it again, only this time, it was slightly louder, "Be still." Be still, Rhlonda. "Be still and know that I am God." Those words were all too familiar to me. I curled up, sobbing uncontrollably. I knew it was God, but how could I be sure, since everything was such a blur to me.

His words began to echo in my mind. Be still. Be still. If I heard it once, I heard it a thousand times. That's when I sat up in the bed, hoping it was Him. So, I asked Him, "God, if You're telling me to be still, confirm it and make it so clear that I know for sure it's from You. Amen"! I laid back down, head on the pillow, and "be still" continued to whisper in my ears. It was Him. God's hand was rocking me to sleep with His sweet lullaby to me. Before I knew it, morning had arrived.

Upon waking up, I remembered what I'd asked God the night before. I heard His words still speaking over me, "Be still," and just like that, my mind went straight to my husband as I longed for him to be there with me. I managed to get myself out the bed, although I didn't want to do anything but lie there and let life proceed without me. With the strength God gave me, I made coffee and grabbed my iPad to head outside to the patio. It was my routine every morning to spend time with God before I started my day, and I needed Him more than ever before. I got cozy in my chair on the patio and opened my Bible app.

I clicked on the Loop devotional I'd currently been reading for some words of encouragement. Are you kidding me? No way! I couldn't believe my eyes. "BE STILL" was the title of the devotion. At first, I was stunned. God whispered for me to be still the night before, and I asked Him to confirm it. Well, He answered as I had asked Him. Tears flowed down my face as my heart lifted. I sat there, not knowing what to do next. I was in awe at what my eyes had seen. I said, "Thank You, Lord. It's what I needed, and You did it for little ol' me. Wow! You love me that much, God"?

After sitting for a few minutes in both awe and disbelief, I continued reading. The devotion encouraged me to move past the chaos and settle in stillness while God does the miraculous. He designed the devotion specifically for me. In that exact moment, God knew I needed to hear straight from Him and used that devotional as a perfect set up for me. He promised in His Word, "I will answer your cry for help every time you pray, and you will find me and feel my presence even in your time of pressure and trouble (Psalm 91:15 – TPT).

After I finished reading the devotional, I remembered something my granny told me years ago. She told me that if I wanted to be sure it was God answering my prayer, ask Him to confirm it. My heart was wide open, and I expected Him to answer. And for the rest of the day, I did nothing but cry at the feet of God, drawing strength from Him. I had no strength to do chores, eat, or work, so I sat on the couch with my nose buried in the Bible and praying all day long. After hours of reading and praying, barely getting through it with all the tears, it was time for bed.

Sitting up in the middle of the bed full, excited, and drained at the same time, I asked God to confirm "be still" again for me. Exhausted, I reached for my Bible and began reading the story of Gideon. If you're familiar with that story, you know Gideon and I were in a similar situation. We both couldn't believe that God spoke a word for us, and we needed confirmation. At least I'm not the only one who second-guessed God. It sho' feels good to be in good company sometimes. After reading, I prayed and asked God if it were Him; I wanted Him to show me with my husband in my dreams that night. Now, wait a minute. You might be thinking because I filled my head with thoughts of him; it would be natural for me to dream about him. Well, not so fast. I asked Him to show me the color red as well. I wanted to be as specific as possible. I couldn't wait to get to sleep so that I could have my encounter with God (again).

That night, God showed up again for ya' girl just as I'd asked Him. I saw my husband and me in a house or building walking toward each other in the dream. As we approached the entrance to a room, I saw a red cloth on the windowsill. I remember waking up out of my sleep somewhat startled because the dream felt real. I tried to pull myself together, but I couldn't. I had to let the emotions go and thank God right there in the middle of the night. God heard and answered me and faithful to his Word. Psalms 145:18, "The Lord is near to all who call on him, to all who call on him in truth." I called, and He most certainly answered.

That weekend, I left service at church. On the drive home, I had a strong desire to pray for my husband. I didn't know why, but I knew I wanted God to fix my marriage. At home and before I could kick my heels off, I stood in front of the dresser in my bedroom. I began thanking God for my husband and asked Him to help my husband, touch his heart, change his heart, fill him with His Spirit, to have a heart for me, and bring him back to me.

As I stood there hysterically, I heard God say, "Do you think this is too hard for Me? Do you think Reggie is too much for Me to handle? I have some chiseling to do on him. Just be still." I knew. I knew. I knew it was God. I began to praise and thank Him for His presence. Then it hit me. "Chiseling? Did I hear You say chisel, God?" The image of a giant boulder came to mind. I thought of the substance of boulders and how hard they are to break. Just the thought made it seem impossible. If God had some chiseling to do much like a boulder, this wouldn't take a minute. But I was all right with that as long as that meant he would come back to me. I exhaled deeply and left that impossibility to a bigger and possible God.

All that I needed to do was to be still. I needed to let God work, right? Well, let me let you in on a little secret. I looked at my watch (tap, tap, tap) and back up to God a million times because He took too long. But let me reassure you of one thing from God's lips to our ears, "God always answers, one way or another, even when people don't recognize his presence." (Job 33:14 MSG)

Waiting on God

SHHHH....Do you hear that? Don't move. You have to listen closely. Do you hear it? Well, neither did I! No matter what I did or didn't do, God was completely silent after He told me to be still. I thought it was a cruel joke God was playing on me. I mean, He went to great lengths to show me it was Him speaking, and now He wanted to play hide-n-go-seek. What kind of God would do that to His child? All the crying, all the praying, all the yelling and temper tantrums I did, and God was goose-eggs silent, and I didn't quite get it.

Without a shadow of a doubt, I'd heard Him before. I'd even seen the results of past prayers answered before this debacle of a breakup happened. I felt His presence many times before, so why would He just disappear. Not only was my husband gone, but God was too in the silence.

How would you feel when you can't quite hear God or when He seems not to be listening? Well, add that to the waiting period. Waiting in silence; no, I'm sorry, waiting with all the noises in your head, and He's silent. The absolute worst feeling ever and, most times, unbearable. God was fully aware my husband left, so it was downright unfair that He didn't come to my defense right away, right?

Yep, that's laughable. I needed to get a grip, let God be God, and stop with the foolishness. But it was easier said than done. It took me a long time to get out of that rut. I was determined to be mad at God for not talking to me, which was why I couldn't hear from Him.

So, if you don't want to end up like me, do me a favor. JUST STOP. Stop trying to take over the situation. Stop trying to be God (as my BFF told me). It. Ain't. Gonna. Work. God is still God. So, no matter how much you fight, whine, and fuss, He's still going to do what He does when He does it.

The other side of trying to put a rush on God is I prolonged my deliverance by acting like a fool. As God was "waiting" on me to stop and release my control, He was still working things out for me. But because I insisted on wallowing in self-pity, He graciously left me to myself and continued to be God, working out the plans He had for my life. He was giving me hope and preparing my future just as He promised in Jeremiah 29:11. My actions couldn't stop the hand of God from fashioning the pieces of my life back together again.

I'll Take It From Here

Sitting in my living room days after my husband left, I was reminded of God's confirmation, "Be still." I was so exhausted from talking to God that all I could do was cry. I had no more words. My groanings made no sense as I tried to put my thoughts into prayers. I couldn't think of anything I hadn't already said to Him. As I sat there, I wondered if God cared about the tears rolling down my face. I wondered if He heard the many cries I had in the days past. Look, my crying went to a whole other level. Oh, my goodness! I remember pulling myself from the floor and going into the bathroom to wash my face. As I stood in front of the mirror, I looked up. "Now, really, Rhlonda?" I said to myself in disbelief. I didn't even realize I'd cried so much and for so long that I had dried up salt stains on my face. No kidding. And, oh baby, did that send me wailing again. I was a hot mess kind of wreck. By that time, I was D&G, and I'm not talking about Dolce and Gabbana either. I'm talking about doom and gloom.

How much longer was I going to have to wait on God? I was slipping fast into an anxious pool of worry. Whenever I feel something isn't happening, the "takeover" spirit comes upon me, and I do what it takes to get it done. "Look, God, I get it. You have millions of people to tend to on this earth, so I got this." And with the snap of my finger, I took back what I had given to a very capable God because I thought He wasn't moving fast enough. At least not for me.

Marriage Restoration Takeover

After a week or so, I decided to try and put this all into perspective. I was so intent on my marriage working that I thought of chronicling everything that happened and was going to happen. I told myself to write it all down again because God would answer any day now and show up to reveal everything. That feeling gave me a slight sense of peace and a smile on my face.

I began "my" healing and restoration journey because I wanted my marriage to work. I was going to fight for it. I knew this season of struggle was going to bring about the truth, and most of all, I wanted to stand in faith and watch God restore not only my marriage but also my husband. There was a battle within him so deep he was almost unrecognizable to me. I'm a woman of faith and have a relationship with God, so I knew this was an attack of the enemy. The very fact that my husband told me he wasn't or didn't need to go to church anymore (mind you, he said this right after we came back from our honeymoon) was not only odd but out of the blue. When I asked why, he said, "I just went because I wanted to make sure you could get a prayer through; I talk to God every day, so I don't need to go." Talk about my mind blown. I could hardly believe it. He knew how important worshiping together meant to me. Even after he made that statement, I continued to ask him to go to church, and he refused. So, I went by myself week after week after week.

As I sat thinking, I accepted that my marriage broke down. Satan was out for a "threefer": me, Reggie, and my marriage. And his final blow was divorce. Although this was my reality, I hoped that my marriage was restorable. At least, that's what I thought, wanted, or needed. I still loved him despite everything that happened. And even though I was hurt and disappointed by his actions, I was hopeful and didn't want to give up on him. I assumed that he was going through something that he wasn't sharing with me. Of course, I noticed the little "breadcrumbs" of behavior, unlike that of a man who loved his wife. However, I was determined to get to the bottom of what it was. I prepared myself for battle as best I could because I knew saving my marriage wouldn't be an easy task. I needed to figure out what the hell happened to him, our marriage, and yes, even me.

Taking Matters Into My Own Hands

Amidst the negative thoughts and hurt feelings, I knew if I would get through to my husband, I had to develop a plan (I know again). Let me stick a pin right here and have some straight talk about fighting for my broken marriage. Look, I know some heads are shaking, and faces are grimacing at the fact that I would even consider wanting a man who walked out. I know; I get it. I struggled with the idea of it myself. I had days when my emotions were going back and forth like a swinging pendulum. One day I was all in, and the next, I wanted to get absolute revenge for what he'd done. And that was only after a week and a half of him being gone. But, even so, I wanted my marriage, period. My gut told me this wasn't the end, at least not now. There were too many "unknowns" about what happened. If I were to discover the real reason behind my marriage breaking down, I needed to stay and fight.

Going into my marriage, I knew I was in it for the long run, no matter what Reggie and I had to face. I put God first in my marriage and continuously prayed for both my husband and me. I never doubted that I was going to be a good wife for him. I understood and honored God's word for wives to submit to (NIV), understand, and support (MSG), husbands (Ephesians 5:22). Yep, I did it all. The vows to God, Reggie, and our family and friends were to love him, support him, and be there through the hard times. And guess what? We were struggling in our marriage. So, I made it up in my mind to stay and fight.

Although my thoughts were still a bit foggy, and my days were filled with crying, I needed a sense of purpose. I was sick and tired of being sick and tired. With my mind no longer focused on waiting for God to handle this for me, I decided to help Him out. Don't get me wrong; I didn't push God out of the picture. I just wanted to help Him out a little.

I set aside my journal, pens, highlighters, and my Bible. God was silent, so what did I have to lose?

If only Reggie and I could talk again, perhaps I could convince him to come back home and work things out. Standing at the kitchen counter, cell phone in hand, I dialed his number. I paced back and forth as the phone rang. By the 4th ring, I knew he wasn't going to answer. And I was right. No answer. The call went straight to voicemail. And guess what? I was too afraid to leave a message, so I didn't. Crap! I walked around on eggshells when Reggie was there, and nothing changed after he left.

I was afraid to talk to my husband. There I stood, pit in my stomach, afraid to leave a message, so I hung up and cried. After a few more times of calling and Reggie ignoring me by sending me to voicemail, I gave up. I guess God was trying to tell me, "No, thanks, I don't need your help."

Crying was as routine as blinking for me now. I was hardly aware when I was crying most of the time. I practically went bat crazy, not knowing how Reggie was doing or where he lived. I was concerned with how he felt, if he'd told his mom he left, or if his "golf buddies" knew what happened. I don't know why I was concerned with what others' thoughts, but these thoughts consumed my mind.

I continued to call, text, and email. I mustered up the courage to leave voicemails. Yet again, no response from Reggie whatsoever. I hate to admit this, but I called his mom as a way to stay connected with him. She knew what happened, and, at least, she gave me the support her son chose not to give. After many attempts to contact him, I painfully realized he wasn't thinking about me. I'm sure you can agree that my plan didn't work. After taking matters into my own hands, not only was I was exhausted from crying but depression covered me like a warm blanket, and I snuggled right into it. Everything about me and what I once knew about me was numb... gone... drained out, all at the hands of him.

Through it all, God was still in control, even during the silence. But no, not me. I had no control over the situation, and if anything were to happen, it would happen after I'd done what He so graciously told me to do, be still. So, I knew it was time to do it His way. My faith most certainly was being tested, and I failed big time, going back and forth on what I gave to God to fix.

Repent, Yield, Get Out of Your Own Way

One morning, as I sat in my living room (you can see this is where I spent most of my time), I decided to go back and remember why we came together in the first place. I figured this would give me the strength I needed to keep fighting. I needed to remember the good times and even the mistakes to take ownership and accountability for my part. There I was praying, asking God to show me my heart's intentions. I pleaded with Him to show me what I could have done differently to make him stay. That's where the hands of *HIM* (God) began. But not so fast.

Even though I was still a wreck, broken, and feeling emotionally drained, I had the bright idea to jump right in with studying the fruit of the Spirit, starting with love. Studying would be easy-breezy because I knew I loved my husband. So, I started searching for scriptures on "love." Then I heard God say, "Uhhhh, pump the brakes, little lady. Do you honestly think you can just come into My presence like this?"

Uhh, yeah, You said to come as you are, I thought to myself.

"Yes, of course, you can. I've already accepted you just the way you are. But you need to know you won't hear Me clearly if you don't do some things first."

Now, wasn't that funny? All this time, I'd been waiting for God to say something about fixing my marriage, and He called me out. Nonetheless, I knew it was God, so I dared to say, "Okay... such as?" Sitting there, feeling isolated and cut off because His voice was gone, I felt a nudge. Three things resonated inside of me: repent, yield to God, and get out of your own way. I started repeating them over and over and over again. The more I repeated them, the deeper I connected to what God was trying to show me.

Repent

The first thing God was trying to tell me was to repent, and the more I focused on it, I realized I was way off base with my thoughts about the entire situation. I knew what it meant to repent, or, at least, I thought I did. But to be sure, I grabbed my Bible, journal, pen, and highlighters to start digging deeper into what God was about to show me.

In my study, I discovered that the true meaning of "repent" is to "turn away" or change direction from the sin that kept me from the freedom I rightfully have in Christ. Well, what the heck! Why did I need to repent? I mean, my husband was the one who sabotaged our marriage, just shook it off like shit under a shoe, and now I need to repent? Really?

Regardless of how I felt, I needed to push through this area. The longer I sat with repent and dug deeper into the meaning, God revealed that I needed to repent of how I viewed myself. He showed me how I was all over the place and allowing emotions to rule every thought and action. God showed me I wasn't going to keep trying to make this man love me or spend time with me.

Then, in another, I was praying for God to restore my marriage and help me be the woman he needed. I was unstable. I was unstable in my thoughts, the words I spoke, and my actions. In other words, I was double-minded, and the Bible speaks of a person who is double-minded as being unstable. I went back and forth because I had doubts about my husband, doubts about me, and doubts about the marriage ending. Just like it says, I had waves of doubt tossing back and forth in my mind. No wonder I couldn't hear from God. The high winds of doubt were louder than His gentle breeze of peace.

God prompted me to repent in my actions toward my husband, regardless of his actions toward me. No doubt, I had to do something different than what I had been doing. Yeah, yeah, the definition of insanity is (blah, blah blah). You all know the saying, right? But it's true. One of the first verses I read on repent stated, "If you repent, I will restore you, that you may serve me" (Jeremiah 15:19). Baby look, when I saw the words "restore," a sista got a little happy. That's what I prayed for God to do, restore my marriage. Now, we're onto something, God! I thought I had the magic key to restoring my marriage. Not only would God restore my marriage, but we (me and my husband) would serve God together. I now know that I took that verse and made it what I wanted it to mean.

Have you ever repented for something you didn't think you had to because it wasn't your fault? Crazy question, I know, but think about it. Often, we're faced with difficult times, causing us to feel we made things go haywire. As a result, we have a colossal guilt trip that has nothing to do with us. In my case, I felt guilty and found myself apologizing for the other person who wronged me. That's absolutely crazy but true for me. I've prayed and asked God to forgive me for the wrong my husband did to me. Huh? Yep. Perhaps and for some strange reason, I thought I caused him to act out toward me. And because of wrong thinking, I picked up guilt that didn't belong to me in the first place. It's true; I may have played a part in it but not to the extent that warrants me to repent for him. In realizing this, I knew I had to repent for MY actions only where the marriage broke down. So, I did.

Yield

The second thing God said was to yield. To yield means to give way, surrender, or relinquish. But yield what? What was it? How was I resisting?

Ohhh, I needed to give my marriage to God. Okay, well, that was easy because I gave my marriage to God from the start. However, in doing so, I still resisted releasing total control to Him. I tried my best to hold fast to my way of fighting for my marriage, even though it wasn't working. I knew God was in control, but I wasn't really ready for Him to have that level of control to the point that if He said, "It's over," I'd be one hundred percent okay with it. Nope. I, frankly, couldn't let go and let God. I wanted a specific outcome, and if I continued fighting (in my strength), my husband would realize how much I loved him and come back home. But that's not yielding to God. It's called being stubborn and controlling. Let's go ahead and say that it won't work, especially when God was trying to do something else in my life.

Also, yield meant to be careful. I was to proceed with caution because I couldn't see down the road. My heart and eyes were fixed on what was right in front of me, and even that was clouded by bitterness, hurt, and confusion. God was nudging me to be careful how I conducted myself and the actions I took moving forward. In essence, if I wanted God to work this out His way and in His timing, I needed to tread lightly (not make an assumption about things) and replace my control with trust in Him to do what only He was able to do.

Let me make a point about "surrender." Let's be real here. My marriage and my heart broke into pieces. How was I going to surrender them to God? My heart was gone, barely beating. My marriage was in shambles and what seemed to be unrepairable at that time. What was I supposed to do? I wasn't ready to surrender my marriage to God. I wanted to fight for it, not give up on it. But that's not what He tells us in the book of Joshua. He says, "Now then, throw away your foreign gods that are among you and yield (surrender) your hearts to the Lord God, God of Israel (24:23)." Wow! There was no way I could ever view my marriage as "foreign." But, could it be possible that God did? Everything that happened before my husband left seemed foreign to me. His actions toward me, words he spoke to me, his cold presence around me were all foreign soon after we returned from our honeymoon in 2015. I couldn't see it back then because I flat out overlooked all the signs and was hell-bent on the marriage staying intact. Could it be I surrendered to my husband and not God?

Get Out of the Way (mine that is)

Lastly, God wanted me to GET OUT OF MY OWN WAY! Whew.

There were several areas I needed to get somewhere and sit down. I needed to get myself out of the way of my negative thinking, doing nothing (God said to be still; I'll come back to that later), not trusting Him, and my selfish desires for my marriage. Now, I'm not sure if anyone else struggles with getting out of their own way, but I sure did. Listen, I was so fixated on my marriage that I began losing myself in the process. I started second-guessing things I typically would be very clear about.

I found it difficult for me to shake thoughts I would've hardly given energy or attention to before. I was in my own way, and God's too, for that matter.

Early on, I heard God tell me to be still. When I heard it, I immediately reached for my Bible and searched scriptures on being still. "You will not have to fight this battle, take up your position, stand firm and see the deliverance the Lord will give you" (2 Chron 20:17). The Message Bible says it like this, "You won't have to lift a hand in this battle, just stand firm... watch God's saving work for you take shape." Reading these scriptures gave me assurance, but only for a moment, as I got back in the way, but I never pushed the scriptures entirely out of mind.

God is consistent with His Word because I later saw His hand in battle unfold before my very eyes. Getting out of your own way requires enough faith to let it be what it's going to be. Admittedly you couldn't have told that to me while I was going through. I struggled with taking my hands off of the situation because I didn't see any results yet (after three weeks). We know how we are. I say "we" because most of us want God to show up and show up now. We want the battle to be over and bloody for the other. We'll say something like this: "While You're at it, God, smite the enemy and I mean kill him dead, Jesus. You said in Your Word that You would. Oh, and Lord, one more thing... bless me and take all the pain away. In Jesus' name, Amen!" Ya'll know it's true. Seriously though, taking my hands off would have meant that I accept the marriage as it was, do nothing, which went against everything in my being, and let God have full control. At least I was honest enough to say I just wasn't there. At least, not yet.

As God held my hand through these three areas, I knew He was speaking. The love He filled me with was strange but comforting. Strange because I realized I'd never felt His love like that before. As broken as I was, I no longer felt alone. I felt

God lifting me up, dusting me off, and sitting me down because He was about to do some work on ME (not my marriage). And even as I felt empty when my husband left, I knew in God's presence was where I needed to be. No, I wanted to be. I had no one else but Him.

So, I thought about repenting. Yep, I can do that. I thought about yielding. Of course, I had to give this to Him. Then there was getting out of my own way, and that was where I still struggled. How was I going to accept my marriage being over? Nope, I couldn't do it. Since I wasn't, God may have told me, "Alright, I have no problem showing you who I AM. Let's go." And there I was, crying and stomping along with my hand in His.

Got Fruit?

But the fruit of the Spirit is love, joy, peace, forbearance, kindness, goodness, faithfulness, gentleness and self-control. Galatians 5:22

Something was going on during this time of God being silent. Multiple days straight, I found myself searching for answers, drawn more and more to feed off His Word. My Spirit was on the verge of being depleted. Everything I thought I knew about God was somewhat of a blur. My Spirit was lacking all the nutrients it needed to survive during this time, so for the next couple of weeks, all I had the desire to do was read my Bible, devotions, and pray.

But why was He still so silent? I needed, no, I longed for God to speak. I needed direction. I needed understanding. I needed to feel anything other than hurt and betrayal. He was on hiatus from speaking to me, no better way to lean into Him than through His Word. (I hope ya'll caught that).

I still had repent, yield, and get out my own way at the forefront of my mind. I still needed to feel as if I were the one to save my marriage; a self-assessment would help me see my part in this marriage debacle. One morning, during my Bible devotion, I started reading Galatians 5:22-23; the fruit of the Spirit. Despite how damaged my Spirit had become, I needed to feast on God's Word if I would come close to surviving the trauma to my heart. There had to be some comfort for me, so I decided to dive deep into each Spirit's characters to help put things into perspective. "Good Lord, I hope this helps," is what my Spirit was screaming. In my mind, I was hoping this would give me a better understanding of how I could apply it to my marriage, since I was in an all-out war to win my husband back.

And wouldn't you know it, "love" was the first fruit? Really?

Fruit of the Spirit: Love

I've said it many times over my life that love is an action word. I believe it's a tingly feeling toward another person or an intense feeling of deep affection. Ha! Boy, did I have this one wrong (somewhat anyway)? As I began studying and leaning into God's nudging, He showed me that love wasn't how I thought it was. Love is about giving, and not so much a feeling.

Now, go with me for a minute and check this out. If I love you no matter what you do or say, deserve, or not deserve, I will always demonstrate love, right? Of course. But how is that possible? It's possible because the Spirit's indwelling allows me to give love and keep on giving it when I understand the kind of love He has toward me. Because He resides in me, He provides me with the same kind of love I should give to others, especially my husband. We love because He first loved us (1 John 4:10).

When I think back on how I "loved" my husband, I gave him love according to how to treat me or because of how he made me feel. I most certainly used my love against him if I thought he didn't love me the way I thought he should (control).

I had to admit I lacked the understanding of what love actually meant. 1 Cor 13:11 says, and I'm paraphrasing to make this personal, When I became a woman, I put away childish things (i.e., whining, crying, throwing tantrums, and walking away screaming because I didn't get my way with my husband). I now understand I had to replace these childlike ways and be fully mature in love. I thought I'd known love my entire life, but I didn't. I knew how to give affection disguised as love and I loved my husband out of fear. When our relationship went berserk, I recognized his inability to sacrifice for our marriage, and I was short and intolerant. As he drew away from me, I didn't want to provoke him into being pissed off, so fear set in. I fashioned our conversations to be all about what he wanted just to keep him "happy."

The other thing God revealed to me was fear and love couldn't occupy the same space. God is love. Love isn't fear. There is no fear in love. There is no fear in God because He is love. So, where love is, fear cannot stay! Fear has to do with punishment. I was operating out of fear and not love.

I told my husband during an argument that he was punishing me because I didn't give him the money he asked for to purchase another truck for the business. True enough, I didn't give him the money because of how he mistreated me until he needed something from me. Fear took up residence, which was equal to punishment, where his love should have been. But God, in His infinite wisdom, showed me through my own shortcomings about love, His very own love toward me.

I started to see the void of love I had, not only for my husband but for me too. Allow me to take this passage of scripture and break it all the way down. In Jeremiah 29:11, God says, "I know the plans that I have for you…(*I had no clue how everything would turn out to be, but He did*)…plans to prosper you…(*to give me more love than what I had; to grow what I had; restore and increase my life*)…not to harm me…(*no more dismissing me, no more heartbreak, no suffering. No, He would protect, cover me and grant me favor*)…give me hope…(*things that I look forward to doing, the things that cause my heart to beat, something to believe in again*)…and a future…(*new things ahead…the past is OVER*); emphasis added.

God also said that He loves me with an everlasting love (Jeremiah 31:3). Look ya'll, it never runs out. His love for me (and you) goes on and on and on. Doesn't that Word just sound so sweet? His love for us is everlasting. Not everybody loves us or even likes us. But God's love is forever. My husband told me he didn't love me anymore… his love ran out. But God's love? Uh uh, no way. You can count on it to be steadfast.

Fruit of the Spirit: Joy

Before I start chewing on the next piece of fruit, I have a question. Have you ever really experienced joy? Not the "I got joy, joy, joy, joy down in my heart" church song kinda joy. I mean real, true joy. Joy is a feeling of great pleasure, happiness, and delight. Wow, tell me one person in your circle right now who has joy like this. I'll wait. It's gotta be somebody out there with joy like this. And, where in God's name was I going to get some joy? I was mourning my marriage. The marriage death angel was throwing a wake, and I was the guest of honor. I knew I needed to look to God for His joy and refocus my mind 'cause I can't say with assurance I've had this kind of joy.

But, to get the fruity understanding of joy spiritually, we're going to the source of truth that never fails, the Word of God, the Bible. Studying scriptures on joy, I found twenty-seven scriptures from the Old and New Testament combined. One of them says, "Do not grieve, for the joy of the Lord is your strength (Nehemiah 8:10). I read this scripture over and over again. Joy? Pa-lease! From where I was standing, there was no joy to be found. I'll admit, I couldn't even imagine me being able to have joy, not with my husband leaving and starring divorce in the eyeball. So, you know what I did? I left joy right there in the "good book" for a while and decided I'd come back to that one after I was over being mad at God.

Sitting in hurt, anger, and confusion, I knew I had to get my joy back, so I went back to Nehemiah 8:10 along with the rest of the scriptures. The joy I needed wasn't going to come in my own strength, but the strength of the Lord. I was grieving my marriage. I had no sense of joy because my focus was on what I was feeling emotionally. It was half-heartedly on God, which made everything around me doom and gloom. It was right there in the Bible if I wanted joy, I had to draw strength from Him, then I would find it. As I continued, I read an old familiar one that says, "Consider it pure joy, my brothers and sisters, whenever you face trials of many kinds" (James 1:2) and "You will grieve but your grief will turn to joy" (John 16:20b). Both scriptures ignited something inside.

We all know things won't always be peachy-keen. There will be people, situations, and experiences that will cause us pain, let alone causing ourselves pain. We don't want to experience trials, especially those that will steal our joy. What I saw differently this time was God gives us a heads up ("when" you face...) and gives us the end result ("turned to joy"). My dad tells me all the time, and I saw it when I read and reread these scriptures, "Baby, it's already alright." But I tell you what; I wasn't feeling it back then. How about that. It wasn't already alright. I didn't consider my trial joyful, but I was hopeful my grief would turn to joy.

Did I mention I did a lot of crying? I found myself having outbursts of crying or having a crying spell when I couldn't stop. The tears would swell up in my eyes at the mere thought of my husband. Then I read a promise, "Those who sow with tears will reap with songs of joy (Psalm 126:5). I felt His comfort. I knew my tears weren't in vain. Every teardrop had meaning behind it. Every teardrop brought me closer to healing from hurt at the hands of my husband. Every teardrop drew me closer to the joy that God had planned and gift-wrapped for me. He was healing my heart through the tears. Each tear I sowed on my pillow, into a tissue, and down my cheeks would soon be replaced with songs of joy. Knowing that God sees every tear and will exchange them for songs of joy is simply love. Which, by the way, is the first in line with His fruit of the Spirit. Setting my sights on joy was no longer something unimaginable. I sought His Word, and His Word pointed out the truth for me, and it will do the same for you. Hallelujah!!

Fruit of the Spirit: Peace

Shall we move on to peace? Humm, that sounds... Well, let's just let that Word sink in for a minute. Peace. Okay, I have to jump right into this one.

How many times do we abuse our peace, give away our peace, substitute our peace, or never demand peace? Peace is that one thing, no matter what's going on around or inside of you, inwardly, you're feeling good. I mean, Gucci good. That shake it off kinda peace. Peace will allow you to look at turmoil all around you and beg the question, "Really, that's all you've got?" Peace won't let anything shake you even if you're being tested to your core. Now, who else besides me is seeking or need this kind of peace? Y'all know where we're going. So, c'mon to the Bible.

"Great peace have those who love your law, and nothing can make them stumble" (Psalm 119:165. Humph, can't make me stumble. Phil 4:7 says, "And the peace of God which transcends all understanding, will guard your hearts and minds in Christ Jesus." The peace of who? God. Okay. Alright. There's one more according to 1 Cor 14:33, "For God is not a God of disorder but of peace." Boom! My mind was blown! There you have it, folks. That's where you'll find that kind of peace. It clearly tells us that we have peace when we love God's law, and nothing will make us stumble. But hold up, if you read this through, this kind of peace takes action on our part. We have to love God's law, and then we'll have great peace. Not some ol' regular peace either. Then we see that God's peace will guard our hearts and minds. And lastly, if you have disorder around you, please believe God ain't there. He's nowhere to be found.

Now, wait a minute. I could have used some peace going through that mess. I needed freedom from disturbance, some quiet, and tranquility. Geez. You know what, though? I was probably the one causing more disturbance. Anyway, I caused some of my distress during this time, along with the enemy. I hadn't done what God said to do. Remember, in the Bible, where the disciples were in a tropical storm and scared out of their minds? What did Jesus say? "Quiet! Be still!" (Mark 4:39). Now we all know a storm can't hear because storms don't have ears. So, who or what was Jesus speaking to when He gave the command? Let that sit for a minute, and I'll come back to that later in the book.

"Be still" were the same two words God spoke to me when everything hit the fan. Although I heard Him speak, it was the hardest thing to do. I was uneasy because I had no idea what was going to happen next. I went through bouts of anxiety attacks from the thoughts and "what-if's" that rushed through my mind. I had no peace because I had "my hand" all up in the situation, and I did everything but be still. Well, guess what? It cost me my peace.

1 Cor 7:15b says, "God has called us to live in peace." I remember having a talk with my husband (yep, he finally picked up the phone after the hundredth attempt). As we talked, he kept saying he just wanted peace, which was one reason he left. "Skeeeeert. Pump the brakes, mister. Because from where I'm standing (alone, mind you), you're the one who disrupted our marriage and sent everything in an uproar." Then I had to take a step back for a minute. Everything around us was on simmer for a few months, meaning we weren't arguing, since we weren't speaking to each other. How much more peace did the brother want? I knew that wasn't a real sense of peace. Our issues saturated the atmosphere with disappointment, resentment, and inability to forgive. There was a spiritual battle brewing right under our noses, and we just couldn't see it. "Turn from evil and do good; seek peace and pursue it" (Psalm 34:14), but stubbornness had already gotten the best of us.

First, to have peace, you can't worry about things you cannot control. Then, you have to give up trying to control the outcome (ouch). I went through sleepless nights, dark mornings, and worry-filled days because I tried to control the outcome of my situation. God said multiple times for me to be still, but I did everything except that. I created more confusion, doubt, and anxiety that I would have never felt if I had been still and took my hands off the situation from the start. "To obey is better than sacrifice" (1 Sam 15:22a). I was sacrificing my peace to stay connected to Reggie.

I was resisting everything God was trying to show me because I had so many anxious thoughts. One day, during my prayer time, I asked God to search me. I needed to figure out what to do with this situation. I'm happy to share with you that when you ask God for something, and your heart aligns with His will for you, you will GET AN ANSWER! He pressed it on my heart that I was trying to control this situation and that I wasn't trusting Him with it. I heard, "Do you think I can't handle this? Is this too hard for Me?" He allowed me to understand this was way too big for me. It was too much for me to handle; He knew what He was doing. I couldn't stop living my life because my husband left. I had to learn to live as if he were never coming back and let God handle him.

Then God took it to a whole different level. He said, "Praise Me through this. If you want a clear mind, praise Me. If you want to remove the distractions, praise Me. Every time you start to think negatively, stop and offer me a sacrifice of praise." I'd been spending so much time overthinking the worse and trying to control the outcome, I failed to see I was doing more damage to myself than anything else. And, praise would be the answer to lifting the darkness I had around me. Praise would be the tool to silence the negative thoughts, even for a moment. More than that, praise will stop the enemy in his tracks and shift the focus to the Most-High God of the universe. The God who is and will always be in control of all things. My friend, when you find yourself in a desperate situation, go ahead, give God the praise and watch what happens. Everything moves out of the way of genuine praise and allows the Spirit of God to take up residence in the middle of the situation. If by chance, you're going through something like this, and you feel you have to do something, I recommend that you praise your way through it.

Let God be God, and He will give you the peace and strength you need to go forward.

Fruit of the Spirit: Forbearance

After a few days, I was trekking my way through the fruits of the Spirit. I understood love in a much better way than before. I wrapped my arms around getting my joy back (even if temporary). Although I was still fighting with peace, I felt I was on my way to gaining some.

Next came forbearance. Good Lord, what is forbearance? During my search through God's Word on forbearance, I only came across two scriptural references in the NIV Bible translation. Romans 2:4, "Or do you show contempt for the riches of His kindness (forbearance) and patience" and Gal 5:22, which is the scripture above for the fruits of the Spirit. So, I looked up the definition in the Miriam-Webster dictionary. It states forbearance is: refraining from the enforcement of something. In biblical terms, it means showing patience. Simply put, it's:

- holding back from doing something that should or could be done
- controlling yourself when provoked or offended
- not giving the full punishment for something; lenient (ooo-wee)
- and, controlling yourself instead of lashing out

Now, I'm not about to do this one by myself. I need everybody to tell the truth on this one. So, I'll ask the question. Have you been 100% solid on forbearance? Go and sit with it for a minute. Okay, okay. I'll say it first. I've been an epic failure at this one, especially in my marriage and maybe my whole life. I can't even begin to count how many times I lost it in my marriage. Now, wait! Before y'all get to throwing ooo-wees around, let me say this. I stand confidently on my home state's motto of "Show Me." My mouth (Lord my mouth) was something else. I was very sarcastic. But Miss "show me" (I) wasn't like that with my husband.

At the beginning of our dating, I remember he and I were talking. He made a fly ass comment that sent my mind back to handling things the Show-Me State way. I gave him a piece of my mind, neck rolling, and everything. But his response is what got me. Very calm, he commented that I could catch more flies with honey, and I didn't have to be so "hard" or gangster. His words stayed with me from that day forward, as I did my best to be mindful of how I responded to him. I guess you could say I was going to exercise a little forbearance.

Afterward, there were times when a fire was blazing inside of me to give him a piece of my mind, but I sat back and said nothing. I went to the far extreme of forbearance. I didn't share my true feelings and kept it all inside. I played nice and used a soft voice. In those moments, he didn't hear me. However, when I acted like I didn't have any sense and lost it on him, He heard me loud and clear. He hadn't seen that side of me often. But the marriage was on its way to being over when I decided to speak up.

He, on the other hand, was the opposite. He wasn't the arguing type, but he held back things from me. He held back his love, conversation, affection, time, sex, and anything else he could. As things got progressively worse, he would say anything he knew would hurt me, and he didn't hold it back. There was no forbearance from him.

I realized that when people don't exercise forbearance, it's because they don't truly understand God's grace and mercy. God gives us these instead of His wrath, which we undoubtedly deserve. Think about it. How many times have we offended God? How many times have we turned our backs on Him? We probably have done things that we'll take to our graves. But what does God do? He holds back the proper punishment we deserve and extends to us His grace, mercy, and, most of all, forgiveness when we ask Him. That's what God has done with each one of our mishaps or mistakes. Now, that doesn't mean we won't suffer the consequences at some point in our lives. But the mere fact that He is so patient with us and gives us chances after chance without dealing with us as we deserve is enough for us to do the same with each other. I genuinely believe it's easier to forgive others for the hurts and wrongs they've caused you when you accept and agree God has forgiven the wrong we've done against Him.

I'm sure you're wondering what happened to the remaining fruits, since I didn't address them. Well, God was up to something else right in the middle of my studying that shifted my entire focus. Although, I'm not surprised it stopped with these four. These were the ones that needed my attention for everything that was about to take place.

All Out of Plans

Before I move on, I have to stick a pin right here for a moment and share this. One night on the computer, I came across an email my husband sent five years prior, dated 4/4/2013. What's significant is our wedding date was 4/5//2015. The email described how a man should love his wife in marriage according to the Bible scripture Ephesians 5:23-25. Now, keep in mind, we were dating then. The email date stood out to me because he thought about it two years before our actual wedding. Talk about connecting dots just to make myself feel better.

Feeling fluffy and warm inside, I decided to forward it to him. You know, just as a reminder of his words to me. Honestly, I was hoping it would conjure up some feelings for him. I sent the email and sent a text to ask him to check his email (just doing too much, right). Guess what? No response from him. Nothing. Crickets. I had just come out of prayer for my marriage 'cause I knew the enemy was attacking us. You should have seen ya' girl, I walked around, checking the phone and email for a while, just praying that he would respond. I got nothing. So, I decided to go to bed.

The next morning, I called him, since he hadn't responded to the email or text. The next best thing was to pick up the phone, right? To my surprise, I heard, "The person you are calling cannot accept calls at this time; we're sorry for any inconvenience this may have caused. Goodbye." He blocked me. Are you kidding me? He told me a week earlier that he was going to block me if I kept calling him. But damn, I didn't believe him. Sitting there in disbelief, I panicked and cried hysterically. Why was I going through this?

The Long Way Around

I had a feeling there would be something awful about this whole process, but I had no idea I would be in that particular state of desperation fighting through a whirlwind of hurt and betrayal. Once again, I cried out to God for His help. It was me that kept putting myself in those predicaments with all the back and forth. But God. I really believe He felt sorry for me. Trying to calm me down, I heard a small voice saying, "I'm right here. Don't you know I've got this? I've got you. Didn't I say 'Be still'?" Instantaneously, my mind shifted to "get out of your own way." I had to shift my focus, and I needed to do it quickly.

I reached for my Bible and went straight to Exodus 13:17-24 without much effort. Hum, that's interesting. I noticed some similarities with my situation. After Pharaoh let the children of Israel go (husband left), God didn't lead them (me) through the shortest route (this is going to be a long ride). Stay with me, okay? The Bible says that if they faced war (forcing the marriage to work), they (I) might return to Egypt (the marriage). It was clear as mud to me when I read it the first time, so I had to reread it. The second time it read like this for me:

After my husband left, God wasn't leading me through the shortest route. This would take some time to get around this. If I faced war and forced the marriage to work, I might return to Egypt (the marriage).

It became even more clear that God was using his walking out on the marriage. Right there in the margin of my bible was a note below verses 17-18; "to avoid conflict." This note was from years ago, and I had no clue it would be relevant that day. As I continued to read, it went on to say how God led them by a cloud by day and a pillar of fire by night. And there again in my notes, I jotted these words; "God was leading them away from an enemy they (I) couldn't see (I had blinders on). I stopped reading but focused on what God revealed to me. I thought about all the fighting and arguing we'd done. The enemy set itself up against me, and I couldn't see it because I was so blinded by wanting my marriage to work. The enemy had me so set on staying because he knew the longer I stayed, the deeper his hooks would go to take me out of here. I consistently overlooked all the warning signs, and when I wanted to speak up, it was too late; my husband was already gone.

Plan Aborted

I could only think of God protecting me. Did I even need protection from my own husband? What was it? And what did my husband have to do with it? Ah. Maybe that's it. My "plan" to fix my marriage failed big time because it wasn't supposed to work. No matter what I tried, it didn't work. I'd gone through my marriage restoration checklist a million times. I backtracked every detail only to come up with goose eggs. I didn't have another text, email, or phone call to make. It was apparent that my plan wasn't working. I waved the white flag and decided I needed to get up, dust myself off, and figure out how to move forward, but everything was at a complete standstill. Little did I know that God's plan for my life was just about to unfold despite some dark days ahead.

CHAPTER EIGHT

A Hand Like Job

"What I have feared has come upon me; what I dreaded has happened to me. ~ Job 3:25

Have you Considered?

I hope you're familiar with the Bible story of Job. If not, read the entire book. But, for now, read the first Chapter. Go ahead, I'll wait for you right here.

Welcome back! So, did you hear the conversation between God and Satan? Satan basically told God he was walking back and forth on the earth, just chilling, after God asked him where he'd come from. Well, most of us have heard the narrative preached that Satan had to get permission to go after Job, and God granted it, right? Well, I have news for you. That ain't necessarily how it went down. I have a different perspective of the convo, so let's review it again. Job 1:6-12 (Msg):

6-7 One day, when the angels came to report to God, Satan, who was the Designated Accuser, came along with them. God singled out Satan and said, "What have you been up to?" Satan answered God, "Going here and there, checking things out on earth." 8 God said to Satan, "Have you noticed my friend Job? There's no one quite like him—honest and true to his word, totally devoted to God and hating evil." 9-10 Satan retorted, "So do you think Job does all that out of the sheer goodness of his heart? Why, no one ever had it so good! You pamper him like a pet, make sure nothing bad ever happens to him or his family or his possessions, bless everything he does—he can't lose! 11 "But what do you think would happen if you reached down and took away everything that is his? He'd curse you right to your face, that's what." 12 God replied, "We'll see. Go ahead—do what you want with all that is his. Just don't hurt him." Then Satan left the presence of God.

Okay, what in the mess is going on here? The way I see it, all Satan said was that he was checking some stuff out. He didn't go asking God if he could lay a hand on Job or do anything to him. Then, here comes God offering Job up. Not only did God offer Job up, but He commenced to bragging about him to Satan, how devoted Job was. Talk about a setup; that's cold-blooded. I'm just saying, God was the one who shined the light on Job. What's even more jaw-dropping is God had a lot of confidence in Job. He knew all about Job's character, He saw how Job covered and protected his family. That's precisely why He offered him up. Or should I say "volun-told" without telling Job.

Now check this out. Satan knew he didn't have a chance with Job while he was "checking things out." Don't you think he saw Job before God offered him up? Of course, he did. He snuck in a peek and walked away (sorry, slithered), thinking, *Nah, I can't mess with him; God has him wrapped up too tight.*

Upon God suggesting Job, Satan, in essence, responded to God. (paraphrasing again) "Now why would you do that? You know you have your 'hand' on Job. You got favor on him. His family is blessed. His fields and the land are blessed. And Job isn't going to do anything against you because of all of what you have given him." So, Satan presented God with a counter-offer. "I betcha if you take your hand off of him, he'll curse you." And, guess what? God accepted. WHAAAT!! Yep, we see that next, God accepted the challenge. But, but...he puts a stipulation on it. God basically said, "I got this. Do what you want. Do what you want to his household and all his possessions. But, don't lay a hand on him. Don't you just love a good "but God"?

Now, I wonder (and I hope you're wondering too) if Satan would have said, "Aw shoot, that ain't gonna work because that's not really what I want to do. What I really want is to kill him and take him outta here." But God! God said, nevertheless, go do what you want to him, but you have to work around my parameters. I set the plan, but I'll still offer him up to you.

Can you say, WOW! Wow, in the first sense that God offered Job up. And wow, in the second sense that... God offer Job up. I can't begin to fathom why God would ever do such a thing to a guy who has been as faithful as Job was to Him. However, on the other hand, we can glean from this that God must have been especially fond of Job. In either case, God knew something that Job (even I) didn't know.

Now I have to keep going with this story because there's so much to unpack here, as I'm reminded of how familiar I was with the "set up." So, go with me now, and let's see how fast Satan swooped down on Job. Job basically had two separate attacks; the first test was with his family and fortune. The second was with his health. Look, I don't know about you, but sometimes, all we need is some good ol' peeps, loads of money, and good healthy bones to enjoy it all, right? Can you imagine losing every one of your possessions in one fell swoop like Job? If not all, most of us would have a nervous breakdown and end up sitting in a padded room somewhere. But, may I inform some and remind others that God sometimes says, "Did you notice (insert your name)?"

Looking at the first attack on his fortune and family, we discover a few things. Job's donkeys were stolen, his sheep and shepherds burned up, his camels and camel drivers were raided. Lastly, while his children were having a house party, they were killed by a tornado that struck the house. What a colossal heap of destruction!

Remember, the thief comes only to steal, and kill and destroy (John 10:10) and Job's first attack happened in four rounds. In the first three rounds of attack, Satan stole or killed his entire livestock, which is how Job made a living. The sheep, cattle, oxen, donkeys, field hands, shepherds, and drivers are all dead. In the fourth round of the first attack, Satan wiped out his family. These were his children or, better yet, his legacy. Satan accomplished two of the three things he is known for during attack number one with Job; stealing and killing.

Let's all be warned; we're not exempt. The pattern in Job's story shows us that the enemy won't just hit you with a one and done and let you go. No. He is going to lay an attack on you that's going to be followed quickly by others. Even while you're getting the information, or in the middle of getting firsthand news of disappointment, there's another one coming right behind it before that one can even cool down. The Bible tells us, "While he (the messengers for Job) was talking," another messenger interrupted the conversation to deliver the next set of bad news. Not one right after the other, but one on top of the other. Satan is swift, and he is busy!

Now, here's what I need to point out about Job. He heard what happened to his possessions and to his family, and then we see his response. Job's response was quite a bit different from mine. After receiving information that I would classify as traumatizing, Job got up, tore his clothes, and shaved his head. Now that's some serious stuff. I got some good hair, and I don't know if I'm going to shave off my hair and tear up a good pair of threads. Anyway, after he did all that, Job fell to the ground and worshiped. Wait. Say what say, huh? What did Job do? We read it right. He worshiped (Job 1:20). He grieved and praised at the same time. Whoa! Now I see why God offered him up. I can only imagine Satan thinking, *Who is this guy? Humph.*

Reading just a little bit further, God offered up Job a second time. Again, the same scenario occurs. God asked Satan what he'd been up to. Satan gives the same exact response. God gives the same offer of Job. Seeing that Job didn't budge when his fortune and family were gone, Satan suggested Job's health would be the thing that would make him curse God. And how does God respond? You guessed it. He told Satan to do whatever he liked, but he couldn't kill him. The Bible tells us the second attack was Job's health (Job 2:7-8). Job was inflicted with sores, ulcers, and scabs from head to toe. Geez. Job, I'm so sorry, guy.

Satan knew he couldn't kill Job, so he did the next best thing he could by trying to destroy Job. He was successful in stealing his fortune and killing his children. He even attempted to destroy Job's body. However, I think it goes deeper. He tried to destroy Job's confidence (trust) in God. But that didn't work either. Everything the enemy threw at Job, he remained constant at one thing. So, let me remind you again of Job's response to the attacks he endured. Not. A. Word. Job said nothing against God. This story is an excellent example of how we're to put things into perspective when we find ourselves under attack. God even gives us a glimpse of how it all turns out for Job. Therefore, we should have a great expectancy that whatever we have to face, we'll be restored double for our trouble.

What have you lost? What has been stolen or taken away by the hands of someone else? I'd really like to know why bad things happen to good people. Have you ever had your own Job experience? Well, it most certainly happened to me. And, it was at the hands of my husband. Or was it? (Sigh.) If only I could have been so disciplined like Job.

My Name Ain't Job

I didn't know I was about to have my very own "Job" experience. I was sure I heard God say that He had some "chiseling" to do on my husband's heart. Well, I would soon find out that it was actually my heart that needed jackhammering. Little by little, as I spent more time with God, I began to understand the why behind certain things, although I had no clue what God was doing. I was so engrossed with my marriage falling apart, I started thinking God was "punishing" me. Everything was being snatched up like wild weeds. My career, my husband, my money, and my good sense, for God's sake, was all included in Round 1 of the Rhlonda takedown! The only thing left was my house (MY HOUSE!). It was all being stripped away. The only thing left was God and me. You might be thinking that was a good thing. Ha! Yeah right. I didn't because I just wanted my "stuff" back.

"What's next, God? What have I done for you to allow this to happen? Hey...hey God. My name ain't Job. You know that, right?" Don't you say I'm guilty, but tell me what charge you have against me (Job 10:2)? Angry at God, I screamed, "God, are you serious right now? Are you really going to let this happen? I thought you took care of those who follow you." In my living room, I shook my fist at God, yelled at the top of my lungs, and pointed my finger of blame at Him for my life completely falling apart. Not only apart, but into a thousand pieces. Undoubtedly, the Lord saw everything I was going through. So, why didn't He stop it? Why didn't He shake the crap out of my husband and make him love me? Why didn't God make him stay? Or better yet, make him PAY! Why God? Why?

Unlike me, in light of everything Job suffered, he never charged God with wrongdoing. Well, I'm sorry. I needed someone to blame. And I know I'm not alone. When something terrible happens, the first thing we do is look for someone to blame. Ya'll know how it sounds, "This happened because of that. They did so and so." We stomp right into a "ta-hissy fit stank tantrum" because we believe we didn't deserve it, and it's everyone else fault. Why? Because we're all up in our feelings. We're governed by our emotions. When something hurts us, we feel it. But Job did the exact opposite. He grieved. But he praised God at the same time. There's only one reason I can think of that enabled him to react how he did. Because he wasn't stuck on possessions, he was stuck on praise. He wasn't stuck on his family. He was stuck on faith. He was praising God and had faith in God; that's how. Unfortunately, my focus was elsewhere.

I Blame "him" and HIM

Words can't explain how frustrated I was toward God for the state my entire life was in. Maybe you're one of those people who can't admit they've been mad at God. Well, I'm sorry, my good Christians. I can say I have on several occasions. Let me not forget how angry I was at all His rules and regulations I had to follow. Oh yeah, I was piling it on God. The guilt I felt from not keeping His "rules" felt like punishment, and He was against me.

On the one hand, Jesus tells us all you have to do is ask in His name, and it will be given to you. On the other hand, God speaks about His sovereignty, and He does what He wants to do when He wants to do it. That seemed like a contradiction of some sort. Yes, I believed He could do all things. And to deliver was undoubtedly one of the things He should have done without delay for me. He should have stopped me from leaving my job and from arguing with my husband. He should have. Should have. Should have. God should have stopped it all. But, He didn't. He couldn't. He couldn't because He doesn't step in to stop us from making choices. He "allowed" it for reasons I knew little about. Nor did I know anything about what He was preparing to show me. But before I get into that, let me get some things off my chest.

I wasn't just mad at God; I was also bitterly furious with my husband after realizing my plan of getting him back wasn't working. The thoughts I worked so hard a week ago to get over returned out of nowhere. His ill-treatment toward me, the eleven times he walked out after an argument, the offensive words he spewed at me, and most of all, the red flags to which I did nothing for his sake. I blamed him for it all. I blamed him for not being man enough, for lying about supporting my decision to leave my job, for planning his great escape, for being selfish, inconsiderate, and, most of all, a con. Yep, I said it. He was a liar, a thief, and a cheat. As I considered the fact I was alone and without him, it was devastating, and he and God were to blame for it all.

I'll admit it felt pretty good getting that all out. But, more and more, God showed me He wasn't responsible for what happened; I was. It was my decision to leave my career behind, along with every other decision I made during my marriage, for whatever reason. The good thing about it all, God, in His unfailing love, showed me even though I made those choices, He would use them all and work them together for my good (Romans 8:28). I couldn't blame God for every wrong decision I made, no matter how things turned out. However, I could rely on God's promise to take my decisions and mistakes and use them to weave them into the entire tapestry of my life. That's what He did for me, and I'm confident He will and can do the same for you.

Maybe My Name Is Job?

Going back to the story of Job, he said, "What I have feared has come upon me; what I dreaded has happened to me" (Job 3:25). Dang it, I don't really want to admit this. However, throughout my marriage, I had a nagging feeling that my husband would leave me one day. His decision not to make time for me and our marriage was clearly a warning sign resulting in dismissive or unconcerned actions toward me. Each time he pushed me away, I knew I would end up alone. I tried to prepare myself for his leaving.

Thinking back on the numerous times he walked out on the marriage, there was no evidence to support the thought that he wouldn't walk out for good. The only difference with the previous times he left was he knew I would move on without him. He knew I had the resources and the wherewithal to survive. He also knew if he left, it wouldn't be as impactful because I didn't need him. He needed me to be dependent upon him and, most of all, in a vulnerable state. When he saw the opportunity, he dropped me quick, fast, and in a hurry, as some folks would say.

I had negative thoughts buried in my heart. Anytime I spoke of my marriage, it would be accompanied by the words, “I can’t, I don’t, nothing is ever, I won’t have, etc.” I fed my mind with all that junk, and it only left me feeling depleted, ashamed, and frustrated. So, there I was, just like Job, getting the thing I feared the most: him leaving.

I resonate with Job deeply. Job defended himself after his friends accused him of doing something wrong to undergo such agony and destruction. The only difference was it wasn’t coming from my friends or loved ones. I was in a debate with myself. My thoughts brought judgment upon me. The longer I thought about how God could allow this to happen to me, the more grievances piled up. Just like Job, “I loathe my very life; therefore, I will give free rein to my complaint and speak out in the bitterness of my soul” (Job 10:1). I couldn’t believe my life took this turn. I was right on the heels of turning 50 years old with just one more year to go. But God decided to shake some things up, and there had to be a reason for all of this. What had I done to deserve this? Job was brave enough to ask God, so I thought to give it a try myself.

“God, show me my sins! I have served you all my life. I have given my life and my children to you because I trusted that you would take care of me. I placed this man before you even before we exchanged vows because I couldn’t do it alone. I know you saw all the things he’s done and heard all the vile words he’d spoken against me, YOUR CHILD! This marriage breaking down is his fault. He was the one who stopped going to church, not me. He put golfing before you and me. So, you tell me, what did I do to deserve this? Why aren’t you punishing him? That’s my case, God, and I know you will show me I’m right.” Nobody can talk wrong about me in this marriage. If they can, I shut my mouth and go about my business. (Job 13:18-19).

I cannot tell you how long I stayed in this state of frustration. My thoughts were just like Job's friends. They kept trying to justify the reason for things being as they were. And just like Job did everything he could to defend his position and ensure his integrity was intact, I too had to stake my claim in knowing this wasn't my fault, and I wasn't going down without a fight. And just as God was silent with Job for 37 chapters until he decided to speak, it was no different from me either. God wasn't saying a word. No matter how much I pleaded my case, it seemed as if it fell on deaf ears.

I didn't know why God wasn't responding. I did all the things the preachers told me to do; call on the name of the Lord, seek God's face, and cast your cares on Him. Been there, done that, got the t-shirt, and it's worn out! Still, there was no one coming to my rescue. Not God. And definitely not my husband. The silence was so loud that it made me go further into frustration, hopelessness, agony, and shame. What's even sadder, I didn't want to do life anymore. Then this happened...

"Psss... hey, c' mere. I have something to tell you. Awe, don't be afraid. It's me... The Accuser!"

CHAPTER NINE

Hand of Darkness

"Yell a loud no to the devil and watch him scamper.
Say a quiet yes to God and he'll be there in no time.
~James 4:7 (MSG)

Considering that I no longer had a job, had no money, and my husband was gone, I can admit that I felt like I had lost control because I no longer had everything that once gave me a sense of security. I continued to pray for God to strengthen me to walk through unfamiliar territory. The firm foundation I thought I had in Christ down through the years seemed to be crumbling fast beneath my feet, and I had no control over the fallout. Although I leaned into God to be my source of strength and comfort, I still felt the need to take matters into my own hands. God was silent once again, so I concluded I was left to my own devices to get control of my life and get things back to the way they once were.

I'm sure you're familiar with the good/bad angel shoulder analogy. An angel is sitting on the "right" shoulder, guiding a person to do the right thing. On the other hand (or should I say shoulder?), is the devil, tempting you to do something that ultimately hurt you or someone else. The bottom line, there is an inner conflict between good and negative thoughts, or perhaps destructive thoughts. As sad as it is to say, our decisions are based on which voice we give our attention. This isn't something we only see on TV shows either. It often happens to everyday people like me.

My thoughts were spiraling out of control so much it almost let the devil cash in his ticket. Everything I had in my heart moved into my mind and out of my mouth.

After my husband left, the different levels of emotions were too much for me to deal with. One day I was feeling down, and the next day I felt a little better. Then there were days my heart was breaking into a million pieces. The weight of it all was, most times, unbearable. I constantly thought the worse. I felt like I was dealing with the worse thing life could bring to my doorstep, but then I compounded those feelings and added many negative thoughts to go along with them. I was a wreck. And I couldn't let anyone know about it because that would be embarrassing. So, I dealt with it by journaling to get the emotions out.

However, most times, that didn't work. Instead, I talked myself into a deep black hole of despair. As I replayed all the negative junk and convinced myself of things I knew weren't right, and I started believing everything my husband said to me and about me. Then, I started to utter them out loud. The more I accepted those thoughts, the easier it became to rationalize his actions and speak on them. Of course, I knew the excuses he gave me weren't true, but I somehow convinced myself they had to be; why else would he have left. And please don't get the impression I'm saying I was the cause of him leaving. Of course, I wasn't the cause. However, what I'm saying is my deep depressing thoughts manifested a swift and false-reality of what was actually true.

Yes, I experienced what I like to call "the shoulder battle."

The Shoulder Battle

The Bible is clear that we should be alert because the enemy is prowling around like a roaring lion looking for someone to devour (1 Peter 5:8), and I've heard it preached. I've practically heard it my entire life. Unbeknownst to me, Satan had me on his radar as if I were an imminent threat to him and his whole army, and perhaps I am. But the day my husband left his post, not only was I vulnerable to Satan's subtle and sometimes flat-out deadly tactics, but I was also exposed and unprotected. The head of protection was gone, and now the enemy could finish his work in destroying me, as I was without backup.

As stated earlier with Job, the enemy has three goals in mind for us: steal, kill, and destroy (John 10:10). He had all three tickets with my name on them. He stole my livelihood, destroyed my marriage, and now the only thing left was to hover the idea that I would be better off dead until he killed me. Although that may seem somewhat straightforward to say, it was true. But he didn't come right out and say he was going to kill me. No, he was slick about it. He was low key with his alluring thoughts. He dressed it up so pretty that he almost made me believe it was my idea.

A little over a month after my husband left, I recall sitting in my living room. I was numb to everything around me, which wasn't much. I couldn't think clearly anymore because every thought my brain could hold during that time collided with the other. Thoughts were running over, running together, running in, and running out. I couldn't think straight.

I hadn't moved from the couch in days, and I hadn't eaten any food since God knows when. There I was sitting with no music playing (which I generally do). The TV wasn't on. It was complete silence hovering throughout the entire house. So, what was I doing? I'm not 100% sure, but I'm slightly confident I was thinking about "him." Because that was my thing, that's what I did then. And as I sat there thinking about him and my marriage, I could feel that I was on the verge of a psychotic break as I repeated every word I heard my husband say about me and us. Most of them were vile, disrespectful, and degrading toward me. And all I could do was press "replay" over and over again in my head.

Replaying the vile comments was where Satan wanted me and his opportunity to cash in the last ticket he had on me, the "kill ticket." The more I replayed those words, I heard something different. Now I have to play this out exactly as it happened; so, go with me for a minute. Let the shoulder battle begin.

"I have something to tell you… about your husband," said the accuser.

"Uh… nope. I'm not about to do this," I thought.

"You know this is all your fault because you drove your husband away. And he ain't never coming back."

No, no, no, Lord, I…

"Your husband would still be here if it wasn't for you'."

"Lord… please God…"

"Ha, you think HE hears you? If He did, you wouldn't be here. He doesn't care about you."

"God, I know you hear me. Pleeeeeeze, Lord, my mind, my mind… help my mind."

"He doesn't love you, and neither did your husband."

"Help me, Lord… please God… help my mind. Free my mind. Help my mind."

"You meant nothing to him. He left you with nothing. Now whatcha gonna do?"

"God, please... I know you hear me. Help me... touch my mind."

"Shhh... be still," said a small voice.

"He ran you and everything you had into the ground, and you didn't even see it coming."

I continued to cry out to God, "Lord, help me. Help me, please." As I lay on the couch with my face cupped in my hands, I heard, "Focus on me. I got you. Do not fear."

"God ain't got you. You may as well get over it; ain't no reason to keep going on like this."

Hysterically, I cried because I knew Satan was so close to me, and I had never felt anything so heavy and dark like it before. I did everything I could to shake myself or wake myself from a bad dream, but it continued.

"Whatcha gonna do... you gonna stay like this... this is how you want to live or better yet die? Without him? Without your husband? IF you really want to be with him, just listen to me."

God... God... God, please, God.

"Trust in me. I won't leave you. You won't lose. You can hear my voice, my voice, my voice. Listen to my voice."

Listen, ya'll, I lived through that battle in my mind. The enemy said these things to me. It's something I'll never forget. I was at my lowest, and at that very moment, it was an open season for Satan to come in and take me out. It was clear that the enemy was whispering death into my mind. Now, I have no idea how long this back and forth went on, as he tried to convince me I was a failure and things about my husband and business. But I remember that dialog for sure during that battle. It was surreal, and I knew it was NOT okay, and neither was I. Once I realized that he wouldn't let go of me, I cried out one name; Jesus!

"JESUS, JESUS, JESUS. Help me, Jesus! Please save me. JESUS. No, no... Satan, you're a liar. You can't have me. You can't have me. Take your hands off my mind. Jesus, I need you. Please God, I need you."

At that moment, I felt God's presence as I rocked myself back and forth on the couch. I remembered something my pastor told us during one of his sermons. He said, "I will not die. Not now and not like this." I felt it immediately. I had to declare that I wasn't going to die and certainly not like that. Almost immediately, I felt myself jump, like someone shaking me. My eyes popped open, and I looked around the room and sat there in disbelief for a second. Never have I been so scared in my life. But at the same time, I experienced and knew that demons tremble at the name of Jesus. Satan didn't win. He can't, and he won't ever win.

There are two things I know about the name Jesus according to the Bible. First, anyone who calls on the name of the Lord shall be saved (Acts 2:21), and second, demons will beg for Christ to leave them alone when they see Him coming (Mark 5:7 TPT). Somewhere during the battle in my mind, I remembered to SAY His name. I started whispering, "Jesus. Jesus, help my mind." The more I said it, the louder the enemy became as he threw out his accusations. I also heard him tell me my husband was cheating on me, and I would never be successful in business. I heard him tell me I may as well kill myself cause there's nothing to live for. It was real. I have goosebumps writing it now. But, when I cried out to heaven, God cut off the enemy's voice. I could hear God say, "Listen to my voice. You are mine, and mine hear my voice. You are loved, and I will get you through this. I just need you to be still and know that I am God.

Now, how happy do you think I was when that was over? Happy as a baby chewing on a teething ring.

After the "shoulder battle," my state of mind was in a much better place. But, my heart, not so much. I still longed for the return of my husband as I continued to ask God to bring him back. I even had a strange request for God to show me what my husband was up to. Things still didn't make sense about his leaving, and I was more than curious to know what the deal was. So, as I waited for God to show me, I needed to shift my focus to my business. I leaned into the strength I had left and focused on moving ahead.

Employment Verification

By this time, my business was established. I was in a steady cadence of work and feeling pretty good. Working had become a pleasant distraction from crying all day. Right in the middle of working, I received a phone call from a gentleman from a finance company. After he introduced himself, he stated that he needed to verify employment and asked if I were the owner of Double R. I told him it was, since he didn't specify the company's full name (both of our businesses started with Double R).

Interestingly enough, I didn't have employees, and neither did my husband, so the conversation would be intriguing, to say the least. And just like any other woman who would be suspicious, I decided to roll with it. He went on the say he needed to verify employment for a woman I'll call "Chena." I thought to myself, *Humph, that's a ghetto name, but I'll go with it.* Instantly, my HR skills kicked in 'cause I had to think quickly to get what I needed at that moment. I knew this was a gift from God. It had to be.

"Sir, we have a couple of employees with that name. Do you have any other information you can share with me, perhaps the date of birth or social? By the way, you can share the information. I'm the HR manager"

"Okay. Yes, ma'am, the DOB is blah, blah, blah, and the social is 123 – yada-yada-ya.".

"Oh, okay, that's very helpful, sir. Let me search my system here. Just a moment. Uh, do you have an address on file?"

"I sure do; it's 123 ABC St."

"Oh, I'm sorry, I need the entire address please."

"Of course, the city is "somewhere" Texas, 12345."

"Awesome. Now, what's the date you need to verify?"

"Uh, yes, ma'am, it says she started working for you all in May 2015."

"Humph, okay. And what is she trying to purchase?"

"Oh, she's trying to get a car financed, so we need to verify her income and start date."

"Okay, thanks. Well, here's what I'm gonna do. I'm going to give my husband a quick call to confirm and make sure we have the right woman; I mean employee. Can I call back in, let's say, ten minutes? Would that be okay?"

"Oh yes, ma'am, I sure appreciate your help."

"No, honey, I appreciate you. I'll call you right back."

I couldn't believe it. The guy handed me the information, just like that. I had everything I needed in the palm of my hand. The only thing to do was to figure out how to use it. Right before I was about to pick up the phone, I felt the biggest kick in my gut. Why would it happen that I got the call and not my husband? How did the guy get my number? Indeed, if they needed verification from my husband, they would have his number, right? Also, our business information had never been associated with it. So, what in the world was going on? What did any of this have to do with me?

I knew I had to call my husband, but I searched Google to look her up before I did. There was a profile picture of her from a social media app. As I sat contemplating what just happened,

I knew I needed to keep a record of her face because I was sure she would pop up somewhere later down the line.

After searching the internet, I called my husband to question him about the "woman" working for him. I started the conversation very casually. In other words, I kept my cool. I explained I received a call and wanted to run it by him. I told him about the verification but didn't mention the woman's name. Initially, he acted as if he didn't know what I was talking about when asked if he had "employees" working for him. He started asking me questions about the interaction, but before I answered, I hit him with, "Hey, who is "Chena"? When he heard her name, he was stumbling over his words. He wasn't expecting me to say her name. "Where you get that name from? How you come out the blue with that, and uh, what you are talking about?" I told him he had one more chance to answer, or I would find out for myself. He gave me some lame excuse that she was a broker he was working with for business. LIAR! Oh, so she doesn't work for you, right?"

"Naw, naw. She's a broker." His response was all I needed. I hung up and called the guy and told him we didn't have "Chena" working for us. He politely said, "No worries." We both hung up.

A week before this incident, I had a conversation with one of my husband's golf buddy's wife. She told me she saw him in a restaurant with another woman as he tried to sneak by without being noticed. Of course, she stopped him in his tracks and found out we were no longer together. She went on to tell me some other things she knew about my husband that was utterly shocking. I was ill after that conversation. However, after the verification ordeal, it clicked, "Could these women be one and the same? Only God knew.

"Okay, God, what are you up to now? And by the way, thanks for showing me "his" hand." After that phone call, my instincts kicked in high gear. I knew there was something to this phone call because there were what some call "coincidences." But I believe that there are no coincidences with God. Everything happens for a reason, and sometimes, we don't get to see the big picture until much later. My gut told me things were about to heat up, but I knew God had His hand in this ordeal, and I needed to brace myself.

In my quest to take control, I realized I couldn't leave God out. He'd just proven to me that when things are done His way, there will be results. To be flat out honest, I had no idea what I was doing. Even at my best, I couldn't prepare myself for what was ahead. It was arrogant to think I could handle the situation better than God as if He didn't know what was best. He knew the plans He had for me, and when I decided to move Him out, I'd surely make the situation worse. I had to trust God, and I had to do it on His terms, without knowing the outcome.

Now, I was most certainly worried about how I would continue paying the mortgage and other bills. Then there was the car payment note for his BMW, which the loan was in my name. There was no way I would let him ride out of the marriage in style, so I kept his most prized possession.

One thing after the other started happening. Or should I say, events began unfolding, and I wasn't as prepared as I thought I would be. But God was because my husband started calling questioning me about the BMW. The only time he called me and played "nice" was to get what he wanted. He practically begged me for a week to give him the car back. I didn't care about the car, just my credit. God was at it again, relieving some of the stress off me with one less bill I had to pay. I told him to get it transferred to his name, and he could have it.

Over the next few days, when he called about the car, the conversations were pleasant. No arguing. No anger. In my mind, I'd hoped this was a good sign. One day he called to tell me everything was ready for me to sign over the car. This was my opportunity for me to ask him to come back home, so I asked. And without hesitation, he said, "No, and don't ask me again." Feeling defeated, I realized that it was only business for him. He did what he had to do to get the car, and I couldn't see through the bull. He immediately went back to being the con he'd been all along. After hanging up, I gathered the rest of his belongings, stuffed them into the backseat of that BMW, and dropped it off at the credit union parking lot. From that day forward, I didn't hear from him for a while.

Check Please

My husband was working on a three-year contract that started when we were still together. It was with a global retailer. The contract set him on pace to grow the business quickly and put us in a better place. Before leaving, we were making some pretty good money, so I knew he was doing quite well now that he had left. He was able to downsize his bills (get my drift). Well, a check arrived in the mail. This most certainly was odd because he had an account for deposits after he factored in the invoices. There had never been a check mailed the entire time he did business.

Something told me there was more to it, but I couldn't put my finger on it. I held on to the check for a few days because I couldn't shake the feeling there was more to this than a random act of mail being delivered. Plus, a small part of me didn't want him to know about the check as I was contemplating whether or not to shred it. Just being honest. Why should he have money when I didn't?

I finally texted him about the check. He called back. Played "nice" again ('cause he needed something). Asked who the check was from. I said YRC. He said he'd get it later. Then he said, "I'm gonna give you half so you can pay some bills, but I'll catch up with you later." Humph. It was like that. Okay, no biggie. I assumed he'd pick it up the next day. At least he was considerate and offered to give me half.

A week passed, and he still hadn't come by to pick it up, which was most definitely odd because he loved money. Maybe it wasn't enough to make him drop everything and come pick it up. Or, maybe he was making so much money, he wouldn't miss it, knowing he could get it whenever he felt like it. Or, maybe it was time for me to stop guessuming (yep, I made that up, guess/assume) and find out myself. After all, it came to my house, right? So, I opened the envelope. Yep, I sure did.

Now, wait for it. I'm sure you've seen the cartoon where the character's eyes pop out and stretch way out of the socket. That. Was. Me! When I saw the amount on the check, I almost hit the floor. I remember screaming, "Are you kidding me, God?" The check was for $42,000 and some change. Oh, I did everything I could to not burst out crying. But it didn't work. I could hardly believe it. I knew he was doing quite well with the contract, but I had no idea he was making that kind of money. No matter how I looked at the situation, I couldn't understand why he wouldn't help with the bills. Things were starting to make sense regarding his quick exit. If nothing else, it explained why he insisted our bank accounts stay separate.

Another week later, he called to tell me he was coming to pick up the check. This was the first time I would see him since he left the house, and my stomach was in a knot. I wasn't sure if I was excited to see him or up in odds about the check. When he arrived, I opened the door and wouldn't you know it, he couldn't look me in the face. He just stood there playing with the dog. I asked if we could talk, and he said he didn't have time. But I kept pressing him because it was my only time to convince him to speak with me. I made every effort to get my words out, and he shut me down. He said he had nothing left to say. I asked him what we were going to do, and as he stood there, he turned to walk away and said, "I can't think about that right now, but I know I'm not coming back." Without knowing what to do or say, I turned away. At that moment, I knew the first nail was in the coffin for our marriage ending.

I did my best to focus on my new business in the days following his visit. I needed a distraction to keep my mind off what may be ahead. It was tough seeing that he was over our marriage and didn't have to worry about money. Oh, by the way, a few days after he picked up the check, he called me. He'd finally noticed the mail had been opened. Let me tell you, he didn't have anything nice to say. Oh, because he didn't need anything from me. He told me I could go to jail for opening his mail. I don't know this thing he had about me and the police. But I didn't care. He was only mad because I knew how much money he had, and if anything, it should have made him look like an asshole for not taking care of things as a man would. And in case you're wondering, no, I never got half of the money. Remember, he was only playing nice to get the check.

Once again, I was taunted by the enemy's lies, and I worried I would fall back into depression. I had to face the facts about where things were at that point. I had to pivot and catch my breath before I drowned. But, the most devastating issue I had to come to grips with was the possibility of losing my house.

CHAPTER TEN

My Severed Hand

I was betrayed by my friend, though I lived in peace with him. While he was stretching out his hand of friendship, he was secretly breaking every promise he had ever made to me! His words were smooth and charming. Yet his heart was disloyal and full of hatred— his words soft as silk while all the time scheming my demise. ~ Psalms 55:20-21(TPT)

All attempts to communicate with my husband ceased. I had an unsettling feeling that no matter what I was seeking God for in this marriage, it wouldn't end the way I'd hoped. Even though I continued to remind myself to be still, I'll be honest, I wasn't sure why I needed to be still. I had a life to live, and being still was getting me nowhere fast. I wanted to believe God would swoop down and save me from all the turmoil and emptiness I felt. But He didn't. He was silent. He was patiently waiting on me to do as He'd asked.

Over the next couple of weeks, I was being drawn closer to Him during my waiting period. God most certainly was my strength because I was all out. He kept my mind as I continued to struggle with negative thoughts, trying to figure out what to do next. It was comforting being in His presence as I read His Word. Day by day, He lifted my head. The truth of His words was my hiding place to escape the pain deep within my heart. My spirit was going through a refreshing, but it was no secret that I was long away from being back to normal. Humph, maybe God didn't want me to go back to my old way of dealing with things, the old way of thinking, or the old way of how I related to Him. Perhaps there's more to it than I could see. Whatever the case may have been, I refused to sit around and let life go past right before me. I needed God to say something because my thoughts swayed back and forth on trying to make a decision, and I was too fragile to make decisions that weren't knee-jerk reactions.

Take Action

After the last interaction with him, I was left with nothing. There were no next steps. There was no plan in place to solidify him never coming back. Nothing. And that simply wasn't going to work. I couldn't sit around and let this take control of my life. Neither was I going to let my husband dictate what happened to me because of a decision he made.

By now, it's early November, and I was furious at everything concerning him. I wasn't going to take this lying down, so I called and asked if he wanted a divorce. Without hesitation, he said he did. I was shocked because he said it with so much ease. Trying hard to disguise my feelings, I asked him how this was going to play out. Let's be clear; I didn't have a job, no income, and couldn't afford a lawyer. His response was almost planned. He said, "I think if we agree that you won't come after my business, I won't ask for any money from your

401(k). I think that's the best way to handle this." Immediately, I was filled with rage. Not only was he being selfish, but he was being disrespectful. The money I had in my retirement account was built before I met him, and he dared to imply that he could get half of it. Not a chance. I also had to remind him that I helped him build the business, and since he decided to walk out, leaving all the debt in my lap, he should make me whole and put me back in the position he found me when we first met. Of course, he wasn't having it. The conversation took a turn for the worse—the yelling, degrading, and harsh words spewed from both of us. I blamed him, and he blamed me. And we got nowhere.

This occurred a few times over a few days. It was so frustrating. I felt as long as I gave him what he wanted, a divorce, surely, I could get what I wanted as well. Not to mention, he didn't have the decency to file the papers. Additional attempts were made to come to some kind of agreement that would satisfy both of us. But that wasn't good enough for him because he told me my best bet would be to sell my house, which would give me enough money to start over. He said the money should—get this—"cover what I put into it when I was paying the bills."

It took everything for me to keep from laughing, but I couldn't hold it inside. I said, "Are you kidding me? That money won't be enough for me to pay all the bills you left."

When he asked why not, I had to remind him that he racked up over $48,000 on my credit card and I probably wouldn't get that much for the house when it sells." He said, "Well, that's going to have to do because I'm not giving you anything and I'm not signing the papers if you come after my business." The phone slammed as he hung up.

This had gotten ridiculous. I knew he wasn't going to budge on being an ass. It seemed as if the more he could make me suffer, the better he felt. Not once did he consider me and how I felt. His behavior toward me was ruthless, deceptive, and flat-out inconceivable. I left that conversation wondering who the hell I married. He was as heartless as they come. And it was a lot to deal with.

Now, I'm a pretty smart woman. I understood why he was dead set on protecting himself because we lived in a community state. He would have nothing to do with dividing anything with me. It became apparent that he was both selfish and greedy. Everything was about him getting what he wanted. I didn't understand why he would go to such great lengths to leave me empty-handed. It was no secret to him that I had everything together financially when we met, and he didn't. Why was he so determined to leave me destitute? As if I wasn't confused enough, now I had to try to make sense of more of his actions. After struggling with his proposed "fix" to this debacle of marriage, I was at a standstill. Or, should I say a "be still"? And it wouldn't be much later until I saw God's hand in it all. But for now, I had to deal with a crossroads.

Marriage at a Crossroads

Imagine being faced with a problem that needs immediate resolution due to the severe impact it could have on the rest of your life. On one side, the choice is inevitable and will happen sooner or later. However, on the other side, you know the choice may eventually be better for you in the long run if you make it sooner rather than later. Which is the right choice? Which will be less impactful in the grand scheme of things? Which of the choices will ensure some level of stability for the future? Decisions, decisions, and more decisions.

In a state of disbelief, I wrestled with filing for divorce. Even with everything that had taken place, this decision would change the rest of my life. I had accepted that all the fighting I did to hold on to the rest of my life was quickly vanishing at my husband's doing. He had me exactly where he wanted me. He had me in a desperate situation, and if I were to survive, I had no choice but to sell my house. But I needed to focus on handling the divorce before thinking about the house.

How could I rationalize fighting to save my marriage compared to the fact that this man had displayed in every way that he was totally against me? It no longer made sense to force the issue when it was no doubt over. The time had come for me to let it go. Yes! Finally, I'd gotten a piece of my mind back. It didn't take a rocket scientist to figure out I meant nothing to him. Once that clicked, I could have slapped myself for being so foolish, naive, and gullible toward him.

I believed my marriage could be saved, restored, and rebuilt. However, after hearing my husband speak to me as if I were nothing and how he bargained with my livelihood, the decision to file for divorce was the one I had to make. Despite being a fighter, this one was too costly of a fight for me to win. I also knew that forcing the issue with a man who didn't want anything else to do with the marriage would be detrimental to me mentally, emotionally, and physically. The proverbial rat on the wheel had spun around for the last time. To say that I was spent out from all my trying was an understatement. After a brutal beatdown of my psyche trying to decide if I should give him what he wanted or fight for what I knew I deserved, I graciously bowed out and gave my husband what he wanted.

I struggled because divorce is so final. One thing was sure, my life was under attack, and I quickly changed labels from married to "pending divorce." My desire was for my husband but we had opposing views about where our marriage stood.

I believed it could be restored while he had no interest in it moving forward. So, it's no surprise that it was dying quickly. What good was it for me to keep fighting him for something he obviously was hell-bent on leaving in the dust? It also bothered me that he didn't file the papers himself and was forcing my hand to be the initiator of divorcing him. All I could think of was how many times he failed to take accountability for his actions, and I was left to pick up the pieces to put everything back together. Not only did he win in this case, but he was able to walk away with what he wanted, regardless of how it affected me.

Yep, I had to divorce this nut even though it went against every fiber of my being. I had to tell myself plenty of times in a day, "Girl, get over it; he ain't here and he ain't sitting around thinking about you. File those papers!" So, I pulled myself together and did what I had to. Still questioning God, I was finally able to take the step to move forward. By the way, any step to move beyond that traumatic season was welcomed. I knew I was in a storm season of my life. I also knew that somehow things would change for the better. Hopefully soon.

After wrestling with thoughts of filing the papers, I sat in front of the computer, searched Google, and pulled up how to file an uncontested divorce in Texas. The information came up quickly, and I was able to download forms. It took fifteen minutes to complete the forms and three minutes to put on clothes and shoes to head to the courthouse to submit the petition. To my surprise, on the way to the courthouse, I felt a burden being lifted off me. I had a slight sense of relief that I no longer felt like fighting. I'd done all I could do for my marriage, and if the divorce was the end of the fight, so be it. So, there I was inside the office. I handed the woman the papers, she logged everything, asked me to enter my credit card, card approved for $350, the receipt printed, and papers stamped.

"Thank you, Mrs. Washington. Have a nice rest of your day." I stopped in my tracks for a brief second as I heard my name. I pulled it together, all while fighting the tears back, and walked out. Mrs. Washington—not for long.

Upon arriving from home after filing the petition for the divorce, I knew I couldn't waste time dreading over the thought that the marriage was on its way to ending. I knew that I had to continue until I had everything completed. I must say that I was a bit proud of myself because I had taken the first step and filed the paperwork for the divorce. However, my heart was still discouraged by the fact that my marriage was ending. Nothing could have prepared me for the windfall of emotions that were brewing on the inside. Nonetheless, moving forward was my focus so I could put this all behind me. I retrieved the forms, along with the waiver releasing him from being served by the constable.

It was strange because I knew I had no business filing for divorce. I desperately wished I had a lawyer, but there was no way I could afford one, and he surely wasn't going to pay the fees. I started filling out the papers. I drafted my items, but I wasn't sure about his requests. I called and told him I had the papers to begin the divorce filing, and the petition was submitted. Upon asking him what he wanted me to include for him, he said for me to not come after his business, assets, and he wouldn't go after my 401(k). I asked him about the bills that he had remaining, and he said that he would give me half of the balance for one credit card and all the money for the other. I asked about the back taxes, and he said he would handle it. The rest of the money from the house should settle things between us. At that point, I was over it. I said okay and goodbye in the same breath. In my heart, I knew it wasn't fair because I was worse off than I was when I met him. But, at least, there would be no more fighting and struggling with him about the marriage. I accepted it and drafted the paperwork.

Exhausted mentally from drafting the papers, it dawned on me that I was the one picking up the pieces again by filing the paperwork. I was trying to do damage control to ensure this would be a smooth process. What infuriated me, though, was the fact that this was what he wanted. So why was I filing? He disgusted me, and I could tell bitterness tapped me on the shoulder, but it wouldn't linger there for long. I accepted things and decided to move on. What's next on the list?

After completing the papers, I called my husband, and true to form, he didn't answer, so I left a voicemail. I didn't hear from him for a while, which was another way for him to keep me upset. But it didn't work. I knew I had to continue moving forward to pick up the pieces of my life, so I decided that I had to entertain the thought of putting my house on the market.

Before Thanksgiving, I contacted my real estate agent to tell her about putting the house on the market. She gave me the worse news I could hear. Since my husband and I weren't divorced yet, the state of Texas required that the spouse signs a waiver to release the house to the other spouse. I couldn't believe it. Another hoop to jump through just to survive. Seeing that I had no other choice, she sent the paperwork. Now, I wasn't sold just yet on selling my house. No, I was flat out against it. But if push came to shove, at least I'd have the necessary paperwork. The only thing I had to figure out was a way for him to sign the waiver. Lord knows I didn't want to call him once again, begging for something from him.

Ah Ha! He had to sign the waiver to release him from being served, so there's the answer. It was an excellent opportunity to take care of two birds with one stone and sign all papers together. So, I made a final attempt to call my husband and inform him that the paperwork was completed. When he answered, I reviewed everything and told him about the waiver not to be served. He was okay with it and asked when we could meet. Before I responded, I slid in the information for the release form to put my house on the market. To my surprise again, he agreed. I set up the meeting with my agent to notarize the waiver for him and the house's release with his agreement. I confirmed the meeting date to meet at a nearby restaurant, and he agreed he would be there.

Signature Required

The notary and I arrived at the restaurant and sat at a table close to the door. A few minutes later, I saw him walk through the door. When I tell you, my heart was jumping out of my shirt. I hadn't seen him in almost three months. And I ain't going to lie; I couldn't take my eyes off him. As he walked toward the table, I noticed he couldn't look me in my eyes. The nerve of him. He put this in motion, and he couldn't look at me. What a coward! I thought he would've been happy that we were finally getting his divorce completed, but when you know you've done a person wrong, it's hard to face them. Anyway, introductions were made, and I passed him the papers. *Let's get this shit over so you won't have to look at me anymore*, I thought to myself.

First, I gave him the divorce papers. There was nothing but silence at the table. He went through the paperwork line by line to ensure I'd captured everything he wanted. He read through the first page, then the second-page line by line. He looked up, said, "Okay," and slid the paper to the side. I gave him the waiver. Same thing. He looked it over, only this time much quicker, and said, "Yep, I don't need to be served, since this is an uncontested divorce." I immediately got hot under the collar. He really felt the need to point that out. Humph, yeah, okay. He signed the paper and slid it to the side. I grabbed it because it needed to be notarized. Lastly, he read the house paperwork, glanced at me briefly with the look of "gotcha" and a grin on his face, then signed the paper. The agent took the set of papers, signed, and notarize them all. Everything was completed.

I grabbed the papers to put them away as we were about to leave. Reggie looked up at me (finally) and asked if we could go next door to make copies. I agreed. As we waited for the copies, he made small talk and asked about my dog Roxy. "Really, you can ask me about the dog. Just forget me, right?" He laughed as he said, "Well, I mean…"Un-freakin'-be-leeee-evable! I did everything to keep it together. He got his copies of the documents, gave me a strange look, and walked to his car. Oh, let me give him credit where it's due because he did say goodbye.

As I sat in my car, I had to hold my breath. The tears were coming, and I couldn't control them the entire ride home. I prayed that God would give me the strength to get through the feelings that I had for my husband. Hate, love, bitterness, and revenge were brewing inside of me like a pot of good ol' coffee. I was HOT! You wouldn't have been able to tell sitting at the table in front of him, but that was the most devastating experience throughout the relationship. Despite everything he had already put me through, nothing compared to it.

When I arrive home, I stood at the counter in the kitchen. I looked around the house and thought this was the last thing I had left. Now my house was slipping through my fingers too. I'd lost the grip on what was once my security net. I'd lost all sense of familiarity and comfort. My career, my husband, and my house were gone. Everything was different.

I looked down and saw the papers still in my hand. I cried because my heart was breaking all over again. At this stage in the game, it became real. But I was determined not to let it take me backward. As the old saying goes, "It is what it is, right?" Well, not so fast.

I sat at the kitchen table to organize the papers and made sure everything was ready to submit to the courts. The paperwork for the house (check), everything looked good. I look over the waiver for him being served divorce papers and had his signature (check). Then I look at the divorce papers. Once again, I read through them and what he would get. Then I looked at what I would get from the divorce. Under my breath, I said, "You're getting nothing from this man. You didn't get anything while you were in the marriage and you sure as hell ain't getting anything else now that it's over."

As I flip to the last page of the divorce papers, the entire wind was knocked out of my body. "What?" I screamed. "Wait, a blank page!" There weren't any signatures on the divorce papers, not from me or him. I stood up from the table in complete shock. I thought to myself, *There's no way that I'm going to call this man to let him know that we didn't sign the papers.*

So, as I sat there for a long time, everything you could think of went through my mind. I thought, Lord, what in the world is going on? With my nerves shot to hell and a massive pit in my stomach, I decided to call him. The phone went straight to voicemail, so I left him a message to explain what happened that we needed to get the paperwork signed. I waited and didn't hear from him. A couple of hours turn into a couple of days, and still no response from him. At this point, it was becoming more and more frustrating. He's didn't return any phone calls or texts. You would at least think after receiving the messages, he would respond quickly. After all, this was what he wanted, right? His failure to respond went on for days, then weeks. At some point along the way, I just stopped waiting and threw the papers into my computer drawer. It made no sense to me why he wouldn't respond, and I couldn't make that an issue any longer.

Could this have been God's way of telling me my marriage wasn't over? Was God taking back His hand from what I tried to take over? I wasn't sure. But I did remember one thing: "Be still." I said, "Okay, God, I don't know what's going on. I've done my part with nothing else left for me to do. So, I'll take my hands off." Something peaceful rested with me, and I was ready to surrender the situation over to God.

A couple weeks passed, and still no word from my husband. I was utterly stumped as to why he wouldn't respond. There was nothing I could do with the papers without both signatures, and quite frankly, I was getting pissed. I was fed up being on a roller coaster ride of emotions because of him not responding.

One thing was for sure again, both God and my husband were silent. I continued to pray for an understanding and for God to show me the why behind it all. Whatever God would do with our marriage was fine with me, but I needed closure by understanding why this happened. With everything I had going on, I realized I was in survival mode. I had bills to pay. Even though the creditors hadn't come knocking yet, I needed to survive. I wasn't left with nothing at all. And the truth was taking an honest look at what was left and how I could use it to better my situation. Wouldn't you know it, as I was thinking about my truth, it dawned on me I didn't have anything. I had nothing left that connected us except my house. Immense sadness overcame me. I heard my husband's suggestion about selling my house. I knew what I had to do. Now that my marriage seemed as if it were severed, the next battle to tackle was my home.

CHAPTER ELEVEN

His Hand of Preparation

Within your heart you can make plans for your future, but the Lord chooses the steps you take to get there. ~ Proverbs 16:9 (TPT)

May I remind you of a widow in the Bible who had outstanding debt? I'm paraphrasing here. She ran out of resources, and the creditors were coming to take her sons as payment. I'm sure I don't need to tell you that she probably felt defeated, let alone terrified. The one person she relied on to provide for the household, her husband, was gone. He died (in my case, left). Anyway, she knew she needed help. She had to ask someone for guidance. She needed to seek the counsel of someone who could help her come up with a solution, realizing she was down to her very last.

As the story goes, she came in contact with a prophet familiar with her family and was asked what she had in her house. Check out her response: "Your servant has nothing there at all, except a small jar of olive oil" (1 Kings 4:2). Reading this, I thought she was confused. First, she said nothing at all, and in the same breath, "Except a small...." She had concluded that her "Except" didn't hold enough value for the massive amount of debt she now owed. Nor did she think it would be enough to satisfy her need going forth since the breadwinner was no longer able to provide. In those days, women didn't work to earn money, at least not until the Proverbs 31 woman stepped on the scene. This particular woman looked at how big her problem was and didn't consider how big her "except" was. But, isn't that how we respond to some of the situations we find ourselves in. We discount or place little value on what we have compared to what we think we need or need in the natural realm. Very rarely do we tap into our spiritual sight when we're faced with overwhelming situations in life. I was no exception.

House on the Market

I wrestled with the thought of selling my house for days. I calculated cost, flipped ideas around, and even thought about renting. You name it, I thought of it. Not to mention, praying, Lord, please don't let me have to give up my house. But when all of that was said and done, I knew what needed to be done. There was no doubt about it; I'd lost everything else that meant so much to me, so there was no need to hold on to anything that would remind me of us in the house together. To hell with it! I needed to rip the Band-Aid off and start over.

I called my agent again and told her I was ready to put the house on the market. Good thing I had already had the waiver signed, releasing him from profits made. She basically dropped everything she was doing and came right over. Of course, I had to bring her up to speed with my situation, which was fine because I trusted her. She listened and assured me everything would be alright. She reminded me of the process, since she was the one who sold me the house in the first place and was familiar with the area and the price point for my area.

After everything was laid out, I told her the price to list for the house. I took into account the balance remaining to pay off the house as well as the extra I needed. She told me I was a bit low on the asking price and advised me to consider another amount. I was a little apprehensive about the price because I didn't think it would sell quickly if it were priced high. I was in a desperate situation and needed the money soon. She assured me I could lower the price if needed. I agreed, and within a few short hours, my house became an active listing that Thursday afternoon in December.

I had many mixed emotions after listing the house. One of my most significant accomplishments had been ripped right out from under me. I felt forced into the decision, which was undoubtedly unfair. But most of all, I didn't know if I'd have enough for me to start over again. And! And! What would I look like "renting" instead of being a homeowner? I hadn't been a "renter" in years. Hey, ain't nothing wrong with renting if that's your thing. I was past the days of renting (shoot). I was a homeowner and a damn proud one at that. Well, at least... Ya'll know what I meant.

And in those few minutes, I found myself wondering if my decision to sell would be enough.

As God would have it, three days after being on the market, I received a call from my agent. She asked if I were sitting down. However, before I could get one word out, she said, "Congrats, you have an offer. A couple viewed the house, and the moment they walked in, they knew it was theirs. They complimented the great care of it and didn't want to wait or lose it to any other potential buyer, so they put in an offer to buy. I had no words because all I could think was that it was way too fast for the kid. What in the world just happened? She then went on to say, "Not only do you have a contract offer, but they want to give you $15,000 above the asking price." I was shocked.

Please tell me you can see God's hand? Not just with me but perhaps with the woman in the story. She followed the advice of the prophet. She asked for what she needed. And her requests were granted with the jars. After there were no more jars to fill, the oil stopped. When she told the prophet what happened, he told her to sell it and pay off her debts. But here's the kicker: she had enough to live on from what was left.

I know somebody should be screaming right now because I did when I read it. Had I not followed the advice from my realtor, I would have been just like the woman who put little value on what she had. But because she did what she was told, the woman walked away better than what she imagined it would be.

I was able to relate to this story entirely. I will also say that I was in complete awe of God. His hand was all over the listing, the asking price, and the selling of my house. Listen, let me tell you something. When God says that He's going to show up and stay faithful to His Word, you best believe Him. Now, I'm not saying that I was 100% full of faith and trusting God. No, I'm not saying that at all. Oh, but I had enough to trust my agent to give me the right information, and He allowed me to recognize Him at the helm of it all. I was absolutely convinced it was Him. He did it to let me know He was in total control, and He was using my house as part of His plans for me. He showed me that even though it seemed that He was silent, He was still moving amid my situation.

Let me encourage you by saying you have something to work with, even if it looks like an "except." God makes exceptions go a long way. So, trust him with your "nothing except...." You will have leftovers.

******

Feeling pretty good about the contract on the house, I was in good spirits. The thought of my husband still not responding was pushing me to the limit. This was yet something else he left undone and me holding the bag, and there went my mood. The fear of the unknown started looming overhead. Why couldn't I let this man be gone? What was it about him or even me that made me continuously pray for him? He didn't deserve my prayers. I bet you a dollar to a sack of donuts he wasn't praying for me. So, why should I pray for him?

I knew I needed to get a hold of my mind and emotions, so I asked God to show me something. Anything. There was a battle inside my heart, desiring for my marriage to be restored and highly frustrated with my husband's inaction. No doubt, there were times I felt I shouldn't give up on us and other times when I felt deep regret from loving him still. I had moments of praying hard to ask God to protect him and even turn his heart back toward me. However, nothing seemed to work, as my prayers went unanswered for what seemed like eternity. I begged God to take the pain away and give me an understanding so I could have a sense of peace. Fighting for Reggie was all I could do. I mean, at times, I went hard for him in prayer because I truly loved him and everything, and we felt we could fix our marriage despite all that happened. Most of all, I felt great sadness because my vow to God was breaking as this divorce was in full effect. Indeed, I didn't have to stop praying for him, but I needed to switch my mind to the other things happening in my life. Perhaps they would give me a much-needed distraction until I heard from God again, and hopefully, my husband too.

Flip the Switch

I still had time before closing on the house at the start of the year, so I shift my focus more on the business. It was getting easier to put my energy into my business instead of thoughts about my husband. I started attending more networking events and signed up with a business mentor to help me. I must say it felt like my life was shifting toward some level of normalcy. I was up and out of the house, and it did me good to be around people again. The more I focused on my business, the better I felt. Sure, thoughts of my husband smacked me in the face every now and then, but they no longer dragged me down to the deep hole of depression. I made my mind up that God was doing something, and I needed to do something as well. Focusing on my business was the strategy.

As the weeks passed, there was still nothing from my husband. It bothered me immensely, but I couldn't let it take me back to that place of depression. My business was far more important, especially since I needed to attract clients and grow the business. My energy went into building the business, relationships with other business owners, and writing responses to bids for potential clients. I was so busy and focused on everything I was doing that I hadn't given it much thought that the holidays were around the corner. I needed to switch the focus to packing as the days were vastly approaching to close on the house. I also need to take some time to find a new place to live.

Although the pain and unanswered prayers lingered in my heart, I had peace and didn't feel as much pressure about my pending divorce. Things were starting to mellow out somewhat, and as I spent more time with God patiently waiting for His answers and direction, I started feeling a calm come over me. I didn't feel the need to control things, at least, because I could feel God kept me busy and drew me closer to Him.

Continuing to work on the business, I contacted a young lady who also had an HR consulting company. Immediately we connected and started partnering on business and building clients together. Our focus was on local and government contracting, which kept us pretty busy writing RFPs. The partnership grew into a friendship, and she encouraged me to stay focused and trust God with everything going on in my personal life. God knew precisely what I needed during these moments, these next few months ahead, and even more so down the road.

It's mid-December with Christmas right around the corner. I had to reflect on the last few months because there was so much to be grateful for despite the challenges and heartbreak I'd faced. I remember sitting on my patio one morning thinking about my life, and it hit me deeply in my heart that I was still here. The most unimaginable thing happened (at least to me), but I was still here. When I thought about it, I was reminded I hadn't missed a meal. My bills were being paid and on time, mind you. I was still living life as if nothing ever happened. God provided everything I needed through people who would help me when I needed them. My heart was so full. I was in awe of His hand on my life, even though the silence was still there. Even when I couldn't hear His voice, I was able to trace His fingerprints. At that moment, I praised Him because I was able to remember. Just as David wrote in Psalms 143:5, "I remember the days of long ago, I meditate on all your works and consider what your hands have done." I do remember what God had done in those short two and a half months. What joy I had in knowing there was so much more in store.

Before I needed to start packing, I knew I didn't want to bring anything from the house. Yep, I get it. I was totally stubborn and rebellious, but I wanted nothing that would remind me of my soon-to-be ex-husband. Knowing that God had something better for me, I decided to sell everything except for my bedroom and living room furniture.

One weekend, I sat down and made a list of the things that needed to go. I took pictures, priced the items, and posted them to a few sites. Before I knew it, I started getting emails from buyers wanting to know if the items were still available. Some even offered more than what I'd posted. God showed His hand again. He wasn't going to leave me without. During that moment, I knew God was taking back control. Now, I wasn't sure how He would do it, but I knew He would, period!

But not so fast. I knew the Lord would get me through this, but even in knowing that, as everything was being sold and leaving my house, it was yet another reminder that pieces of me was still being taken away. My job, my marriage, and my income were all gone. I pretty much lost my sanity, and my house was next. To put it frankly, I lost everything that I identified as some level of accomplishment or success. I felt like everything was slipping through my fingers, and I still didn't understand why. I knew I had to carry on.

Within a week, everything was sold and gone from the house. Now I was able to get organized to begin packing the rest of the house. Ah, but I needed a plan. Shhh...not another word about, "there she goes again with her plans." This time, I needed to plan the next phase of my life. Wouldn't you agree?

Activities with the business slowed down due to the holidays, so I had plenty of time to get things organized to start packing. It was important to have things in their proper place before Christmas, so I could at least enjoy that time with family.

Look, I'm a holiday kind of woman. I celebrate everything and make a big "to-do" out of them all. Birthdays, holidays, you have something special; I want to celebrate it. Although I was looking forward to Christmas, eh, not really, I'd barely gotten through Thanksgiving because I was missing my husband and wasn't in the best of moods. And again, I'd have to fake it and try not to make things all about me. At least packing would help take my mind from how I felt emotionally.

On top of packing, I had to find a new place to stay. Just the thought of it made my stomach turn. My entire life was turned upside down, inside, and out. My husband wasn't tripping off me at all and moved into his new place with ease. He didn't have a concern for money at all. But for me, I was looking at a 3,000-piece puzzle of my life, trying to put it together again. I felt all out of sorts because this shouldn't have been my life. Just month's earlier, I had it all. And in a moment's decision from him, my life fell to pieces. And the son-of-a-bitch still hadn't called me back yet.

That was the moment I saw him for what he was, a fraud. Yep, he defrauded me, and I was livid. As my heart broke repeatedly, the pain ran so deep I could do nothing but cry out to God. And as the tears flowed down my face, God whispered, "Be still." As I repeated it over again, I became calmer, and the tears stopped. Those two small words kept me present enough to refocus on what was in front of me, which was finding a new place to live.

A couple of weeks before Christmas, I found a rental home. It was practically a mile away from the house I was currently living in, just three minutes away from my sons. I decided on the house instead of an apartment because there were just some things I wasn't going to settle less than I wanted. At least I needed to be comfortable in my uncomfortable life. I decided to pull money from my 401(k) and requested a mortgage hardship since a contract was pending on my house. It didn't make sense for me to keep paying it, so I didn't. And wouldn't you know it, the mortgage payment was the exact amount I needed to cover all the other bills. Now, do you think that was a coincidence? Nope! I didn't think so either. So, the rental agreement was completed, and most of the packing was complete. Yeah, I was living out of boxes because move day wasn't until the top of the new year. I just needed to get through Christmas, and, most of all, I needed God to show up. I certainly believed I'd waited long enough to hear from Him other than "Be still."

******

Christmas had come and gone. The time with family and friends was the only thing that kept me sane. Of course, I put up a strong front to keep a smile on my face even though my heart was still heavy. Thoughts of my husband and how he may have spent the holidays crept up from time to time as I reflected on our last Christmas together. But I was able to keep a straight face and enjoy the time I had with my family. I made it through Christmas unscathed by the pain in my heart. There was no time to soak in depression because I had to make a way to pack up my house and move.

All things were good with the contract, although the date for closing was pushed back. I had a signed rental agreement, so there would be a small window when the house would be empty. Even so, the green light was on, and I was moving forward as best I could. The last three weeks of living in the house were tough. Looking around as I packed brought deep feelings of uncertainty; it was also a cold reminder of what a turn my life had taken months before. As I looked around, all I could think was my life came to a breaking point I never expected. I felt so alone. Hell, I was alone. There was no one there to help me pack up the house or the rest of my life. Now, I'm not saying my children weren't there because they help whenever I would ask. But that's not what I'm talking about. There was no one there to help me as I tried to pack up the feelings I had. I was alone to sort through it all by myself. It was just God and me, and He had me in a room all by myself.

Isolation Room

I'm glad I can admit that I wasn't in as much of a state of depression as I was before. But I'll also admit I felt God was shutting me off from the world. There was very little activity with my business, minimal contact with others, no phone calls, and no going anywhere. Absolutely nothing was going on. He placed me in isolation for reasons only He knew.

It was similar to a person scheduled for surgery. Before surgery, you're isolated to prevent exposure to germs when you're cut open. The surgeon won't risk anything getting in the way of a successful surgery. So, a team of nurses take the necessary steps to prep you and get you ready for surgery. There isn't a time when you go right into surgery. There are preparation and precautions that must be taken to get you ready to be operated on.

God was doing some prep work when my marriage was breaking down. He was doing some prep work when my husband left. He was also doing some prep work when I didn't have a job or income, especially when I no longer had my house. I realized that God wanted to be the planner of my life, and we were starting over from scratch. He put me in isolation so I would recognize Him as the lover of my soul, my sustainer, and my provider. He was prepping me to shift my old way of thinking. But most of all, He was prepping me because I had to have heart surgery. Once I realized it was just me alone with God, I felt a deep sadness and excitement. But this time, I knew to draw close and lean into God's hands.

As I looked around the house and at the boxes stacked in my living room, I couldn't help but question God again. Many questions flooded in my mind. I wondered why God allowed my life to be disrupted or what He was trying to accomplish. I became more and more curious about what He was up to in my life, and I remember asking, "God, You know all things, so please show me, show me how my life right now is part of Your bigger plan for me. Please show me Lord please."

****

The days ahead were filled with cleaning the house and presenting my gift to the new owners. All the packing was done, and I accepted that I would soon be in a new year and hopefully in a new place of peace amidst the chaos of my life. Packing up the house was sad but sweet. I'd made the choice to sell, and there was nothing I could do but live with it. But what I could do was expect God to get me through it.

Since the day my husband left, doom and gloom were my best friends for months. I thought the worst. I spoke words that left me feeling worse than I was before. I even canceled out my future because I put all bets on my husband. And when he failed me, I convinced myself my life was over. But that wasn't the case.

Sitting in my living room, surrounded by boxes, my mind drifted back to him and everything we'd experienced together. I realized even though I experienced some unsettled, unimaginable, and demeaning times with him, there was one person still left: me. He left his post as a spouse; I didn't. He chose to leave; I didn't. So, I took that moment to thank God that I was still there. I had no idea what was around the corner, but I had to trust that God would show me the way. I had no idea how to grow my business, but I expected God to help me take what I knew and my experience and put it to good practice to develop more strategies. I didn't even know what was in front of me. I stood in my living room with tears rolling down my face because this was the last day at my house. Eyes blurred from my tears as I prayed for strength and Him to show me the way. As I looked up and around the room, I heard the old familiar instruction God gave me before, but, this time, He said it differently. I heard God say, "Be still and know that I am God. Wait, wait, wait a minute. There was something significantly different this time because the emphasis was on "I." Then I heard it again, "Be still, and know that I am God." I try to make sense of it and why I kept hearing "I" louder than "be still." I knew He was God and only Him. But it wouldn't go away. I continue to hear, "Be still, and know I am God." I was dumbfounded, so I turned my attention back to the house full of boxes and said my goodbyes. The U-Haul was waiting, and so was the next part of my life.

CHAPTER TWELVE

He Showed H(h)is Hand

He reveals the deep things of darkness and brings utter darkness into the light. ~ Job 12:22 (NIV)

Imagine walking down a long corridor in a building. There are doors along the long and dim hallway. You approach a door and turn the knob, but it's locked. You continue to the next door only to find it's locked as well. The tension within builds as you try to open two more doors. And just as you suspected, the doors are also locked. You proceed forward, and then turn to look back. You realize how far you've come but consider turning around because, with each turn, the doors don't open. However, you decide to continue ahead, hoping that the next door you approach will open.

Approaching the right side of the hallway, you think this will surely be the right one this time. Standing in front of the door, you take a deep breath and place your hand on the knob, and as you turn it, you hear a slight click. You can hardly believe it. The door opens. You're overcome with excitement, rushing into the darkroom, then suddenly the door slams behind you. You stand inside the dark and cold room, but even worse, you realize this isn't the place you were supposed to be. You look around but can only make out the silhouette of a few objects. You feel around the door to find a light switch, but nothing happens when you flip the switch. There's no electricity.

Now you're starting to wonder what's really going on. You thought you were in the right room, but no one is there except you. You turn back toward the middle of the room, and you can barely make out the image in front of you. As your eyes adjust to the darkness, you breathe a sigh of relief because it's a window. You walk toward the window and notice something's covering the window and you can't see through. No matter how hard you focus your eyes or rub them to clear away the blurriness, you can't see through the window. You're hopeful there's light on the other side because of the darkness around you. Feeling the warmth from its rays would be a relief, but how can you break through the darkness.

Frantically, you look around for something to break the window. You find a small hard object as you searched the floor around you and throw it at the window. It cracks a tiny spot on the window small enough for a sliver of light to pierce through. In anticipation, you search for something else to chunk at the window. You find a few more objects and hurl them one right after the other. To your surprise, the window cracked, and there is a small hole where you can see a burst of light shining through. You step back to see but it's not enough to let the light in fully. In full desperation, you look around for something bigger to break the glass. You search around the room, but nothing is there. Feeling defeated, you move closer to the window. With an empty stare, you're saddened that everything around you is dark. But, more than that, you're determined to break free because you know there's something brighter on the other side.

It's mid-January 2019, and I've settled down in the rental house. It's just me and my dog and some unpacked boxes left for me to tackle. I hoped for a new start with the new year, a new outlook, and some new experiences. But unfortunately, that wasn't exactly the case. I still experienced spurts of sadness of my house being sold along with everything else I've lost over the last four and a half months. And it sucked bad.

After most of the boxes were unpacked, and I became somewhat settled in, I started to feel some old feelings of regret, betrayal, and bitterness. It was almost as if they'd never left. I did everything I could to stay focused on business, which certainly helped, but it didn't replace the feelings that began to surface.

The first couple of weeks from moving in were met with the ups and downs of emotional stress. I couldn't believe I was still grieving not only my husband but my something of a new life. Still asking God to restore my marriage, I couldn't believe I still loved him. But I did. And my new normal was something I had no idea how to get used to. God knew I needed His guidance with my future staring me in the face. I had so much to be thankful for, but I still had a heavy heart praying for him.

What is it about me praying for something that I felt wasn't going to happen anyway? I knew in my gut that my prayers for my marriage being restored were already rebuffed, but I didn't want to accept it. I wanted a miracle. I wanted a miracle to reverse the truth that my marriage was over. Most of my time praying was for my husband and not for me. It was as if I didn't need prayer or restoring like I prayed for God to do with him. I was so focused on my husband that I couldn't see if God were up to something with me. What if God were trying to change me? What if He were trying to get my attention for my own good. Or just maybe there was some pruning that I needed that would align me with God's will for my life. Could it be it had more to do with me than my husband? I had these questions often, and I desperately wanted the answer.

Most of my focus often drew back to my husband and praying that God would show me if he still loved me. I secretly hoped God would give me a sign, so I knew he was alright. The very thought that I was concerned with whether he was okay was troubling enough. But I couldn't shake the feeling. I continually cried out to God to help me understand why all of this was happening. Now, don't get me wrong, I had a feeling why it happened. I'd rather have gone back to being uncomfortable with something I was familiar with than to deal with the pain and hurt I was feeling. It's sad to say, but it's the truth.

I was fully aware of the depression creeping in again. This time, I decided to praise God through the pain. God was still silent most times, but I knew for sure He was there. The money I had from selling the house was more than enough to get me through some dark days ahead. He made sure that He would get the glory for being my provider and sustainer during my time of isolation. His hand was all over my house selling, and there was no reason for me to think He would lift it any time soon.

Nevertheless, I continued to cry and ask God to bring my husband back. I told Him to "work on me" until he came back. I figured that would be a fair exchange. At least we would both get something out of it, right? Little did I know what I was asking for. I think God was a tad bit fed up with me and my crying. It's almost as if God spoke His word to me, "Call to me and I will answer you and tell you great and unsearchable things you do not know" (Jeremiah 33:3). Only, I heard it as, "Oh, you want to know what's been going on, daughter? Stay right there and be still. I'll be right back with a little sumpt'n for you."

Special Delivery

Shortly after I made my compromise with God, I was sitting with the kids after dinner. They were just about to leave my house, and I asked my son Jewel to check the mailbox. He handed me the letters, and they left. I laid the mail on the counter as I would get to them later. The next day I sat at my desk with the mail in hand, and one-piece stood out. It was from a truck leasing company and had my husband's name and my new address on the envelope. Now, this was undoubtedly odd because he didn't know where I'd moved, and I hadn't spoken with him in months. But can we talk about the fact he shouldn't have mail coming to my house anyway?

Before I opened it, I remember saying that this had better be no bull-crap because I'm not in the mood. When I opened the mail, to my surprise, it was an invoice for a trailer rental. I knew I hadn't signed up to rent a trailer, and to find my information on the invoice was a huge shock. As I looked over the invoice, I immediately became suspicious. There on the paper was my information. Completely surprised at what I was reading, I reviewed the invoice carefully and noticed the bill's charges were for the current month. This wasn't an accident because the invoice showed his handwritten signature on the invoice and bank information. But what I couldn't figure out was how and, more importantly, why would it have my information. My gut told me there was more to it than just the invoice. As I sat with paper in hand, I felt the rage stirring up inside as I realized he was still using me and now my information for his business that he so explicitly said he didn't want me to come after during the divorce.

That's when everything came to a screeching halt. I was numb as questions started rushing to my mind of what this meant. There was no way he knew where I lived. I'd only been there for a couple of weeks or so. I grabbed the envelop to check for the yellow forwarding sticker. It wasn't on the letter like the other pieces of mail I'd received before, which made it all the stranger. I kept thinking to myself, what in the hell was happening.

As I sat back in the chair, I had to have a little talk with God because this was unquestionably no coincidence. "Lord, show me what to do and while you're at it; what does this have to do with me?" The more I thought about it, the more baffled I became. I just couldn't figure it out. *Check his email*, I thought. *What? Girl, you're going crazy now. You don't have his passwords anymore, remember?* But the feeling was so overwhelming, I had to try. So, I pulled up the email page and starred at the screen. I had no idea where to start. Then I remembered… I saw the words twinkle before my eyes. I said, "There's no way he didn't change that password when he left. Surely, he wouldn't be that stupid. Would he? Well, don't just sit there, find out." So, I took a deep breath and said, "C'mon God, C'mon God, please let this be the right one." I typed in his email address and the only password I remembered when he used the computer before leaving.

"Well, I'll be damned. I'm in." I was in. The password worked. Now, I'm not saying God made all this happened like He's some fairy password father, but I'm just saying, it worked. Take what you want and leave what you don't.

At first, I couldn't believe it and had to sit back and think about it for a moment. *Now what, Rhlonda? What exactly are you going to do now?* Well, that thought didn't last but for a hot second. There was a reason this special delivery landed in my mailbox, and I was determined to get down to the bottom of it all. Perhaps you're wondering if I felt terrible about checking his email. Yep. I sure did for about a good 15 seconds. But what I wasn't going to do was have a freakin' conscience and miss the opportunity. Look now, we were still married. He gave me his password when I was playing secretary for him for the business. Moreover, this was NO COINCIDENCE! So, I put those thoughts to the side and scrolled...scrolled...scrolled.

Email Unchecked

As I read through the emails, my heart beat uncontrollable, and my nerves were at ten. I had no idea what I would find, but that didn't stop me from searching. I scanned through the most current emails, but then I told myself to go back to the day he left. I scrolled back to September 16th and continued forward. Nothing much in the first few weeks in the inbox, so I checked the sent items. Nothing jumped out until I came to October. An email that caught my eye. Then another, and another. The emails were to three different women he'd asked them to give him a call so they could "catch up". The emails were dated three weeks after he left. It was clear he wasted no time putting himself back on the market, which made me even more curious. So, I kept searching. Then I noticed there was one particular woman he'd been communicating with regularly.

Throughout my searching, I discovered the two of them kept in constant contact with one another. So much so that he helped this woman purchase a car, sent her love songs, planned parties with her children, and made vacation plans for the two of them around our wedding anniversary. It was quite eye-opening. As far as I could tell, they were in a full-blown relationship. He even drafted a fake employment letter for her, stating she worked for his business since 2015, which wasn't true because we were married that year, and trust me, she was nowhere around. But to make sure, I went back through his emails during 2015, and she hadn't shown up on the scene. It's called trust, but you have to verify.

The more I searched, the more I knew about this woman. Then, it finally clicked. Remember the employment verification for the woman in the Hand of Darkness chapter? She was the same woman all up on the scene now. This was no coincidence. God gave me a glimpse of her earlier but waited until He was ready for the big picture to be revealed. What's even more intriguing is I'm sure my husband gave the person his correct phone number so he could verify her employment. But as God would have it, it didn't turn out that way; He allowed the guy to call my business phone number, which my husband didn't have. Now that was no coincidence. It was another opportunity that God showed His hand by revealing this to me.

It didn't take long for me to realize he was as deceitful as they came. I continued digging. I wanted to know everything I didn't know for the last five months, especially about this woman. The emails continued over several months and ranged from ringing in the New Year together (VIP style) to helping her start a tax business.

Whoa! Aa-Ha! Things really started making sense. When we were still together, he mentioned starting a tax business with one of his golf buddies because of all the money he could make. However, the more questions I had, the more irritated he became. He finally decided not to invest. Huh, really now? I think he knew that the way he was going about things didn't sit too well with me, and he shut it down, until he could find someone that would just let him run rampant and do whatever he wanted. He was scheme-beaming all along. WOW! You just don't know a person do ya?

Things were starting to make sense all the more. During the moments of reading the emails, I was devastated. To see that he wasted no time moving on to the next woman, swooning her and helping her financially made the betrayal worse, as if I meant nothing to him. I couldn't believe all the time and energy I put into fixing our relationship before he left, along with praying and asking God to bring him back home, left me feeling like a complete fool.

I pulled myself away from the computer to catch my breath. The weight of the emails was too much to wrap my mind around. Much to my surprise, I didn't feel like crying. Sure, it hurt to read the emails, but I had an explanation regarding his behavior. It wasn't the time to cry yet. Not with the feeling I had inside that there was more. I knew I hadn't scratched the surface yet, and after learning about his interactions with this woman, surely that couldn't be all to it. "She" wasn't the only thing I needed to discover. I wished I could have given it my attention, but I could no longer stomach the thoughts of it any longer. So, I decided I was done with it that day.

Throughout the day, my mind shifted back to the emails. I had an urge to find out more (yep, I was nosey), but I knew that I couldn't do it throughout the day. I had a business to focus on. I thought it would best to pick up late at night. So, I woke up around 1:30 in the morning, logged into the email again. This time I decided that I was going to focus on finding information about his business. I looked for every email associated with the contract and looked through the attached invoices.

I saw emails where he requested back pay for thousands of dollars from the contract he was fulfilling. Good Lord, this man told me he "didn't have money." Maybe he meant to say he didn't have money to give to me. Oh yeah, that's it. Anyway, I continued, and there was so much fraud on the invoices with fake names. My mouth dropped open. He even used the woman he was with as a "driver" on the invoices.

Okay, let me give you some background. I had a transportation brokering business, which gave me access to Motor

Carrier's national database, allowing me to check the driver's status by name, MC, or DOT number. So, of course, I used what I had in my hand to verify the information. And wouldn't you know it, the names on the invoices did not register in the database. Anywhere! That's when I knew that there was something fishy about the whole situation.

As I continue to look through the emails, I also saw fake paystubs templates he'd requested from a golfing buddy of his. The paystubs were created with Chena's name on them, which she used to show employment to purchase a vehicle and set up the tax business. Everything that I saw was a fraud, and I couldn't believe it.

Then I decided to check his accounts. He had to have the same account to factor in all the fake invoices, right? So, I told myself, "Give it a try, try his old password. You been on a roll, so why stop it now?" I typed the password, and just like that, I was in his account and able to see the balance from the fake factored invoices. You talk about a deer in headlights. I couldn't believe my eyes. He had so much money in his account, it was ridiculous. Talk about a mad momma! And that ain't the word I really wanted to use but I'm good for right now.

I went back through the entire year of 2018, and I could see the timeframe when the amount increased monthly. Yep, you guessed it, right after he left. Month over months, his account increased by the tens of thousands. I was looking at well over half a million dollars just sitting in his account. And the lying mofo' only want to give me $30,000 to just go away and not touch his business. Ah, but isn't it funny that he made that a condition before the money started increasing. He already knew what he was planning and needed to safeguard his business. Ain't nobody stupid. It's called premeditation, y'all. He planned it out good too. That's when I really got pissed. No, I was furious.

Sitting there, looking through the emails, went on for hours.

I was like inspector gadget in his email, you hear me. I looked through every email. And since we resided in a community state, splitting everything between the two, let's get on with this community email. How about that?

Afterward, I was exhausted and couldn't think straight, let alone check another email. Before the "special" delivery, God saw me clamoring around, looking, and searching for answers. So, he began to pull back the covers on what my husband was doing. I needed answers, and God showed up. I believe God wanted to show me who He was protecting me from the entire time. The Bible says, "Stand firm and watch God do his work (Exodus 14:13 MSG). God put things in plain sight in my mailbox. I was able to correctly guess the passwords that I had never tried before. It was almost too easy as I thought to myself, *Try this,* …and I typed the password and ta-dah! I was able to see everything Reggie did in the dark and behind my back.

The Visible Intervention?

I felt relief for three reasons; God spoke, God showed, and God Protected. I asked God to remove the agonizing clutter from my mind so I could hear Him. I struggled to hear His voice, no matter how much I prayed, sat still (as best as I could), and feasted on His Word of truth. There were still moments when I only heard the annoying sound of silence. Just when I was almost out of gas, He showed His hand.

Then I remembered my husband saying it was my fault because I didn't believe in and supported the business. That was a flat out LIE. God loved me so much that He needed to show me the truth. It was never about me not supporting my husband, not believing in the vision, or not wanting to give him money for the business because I did. I was willing to share it all with him. But God had to show me it wasn't all about me but about the position of my husband's heart. His heart wasn't right. God knew he had it in his heart to deceive, lie, cheat, and steal. So, what did He do?

God put His hand of protection around me. Listen, I was so devoted to my husband and marriage that my definitions of "submissive" and "honor" were kind of distorted. I'm only held accountable to my husband as he is being led by the Lord's standards. I was determined to keep my vows to my detriment. I was willing to give my husband the support and anything else he needed, but God wouldn't let me be taken out like that. No way! Not knowing that my husband was on his way down a path that would cause harm to me, God intervened but didn't reveal it to me until months later. God showed me "his" (my husband's) hand and how He was protecting me.

Moreover, He was protecting my name. My name is associated with who I am. And God wouldn't allow me to define myself by my husband's standards. He exposed every lie that my husband tried to attach to me. And here's the beauty and how important it was for God to expose it. God knew that I started believing my husband's lies. I'd gotten comfortable believing maybe him leaving was my fault. So, God protected me from the lies of my enemies.

I was reminded of a Bible scripture that says, "You were shown all this so that you would know that God is, well, God. He's the only God there is. He's it. He made it possible for you to hear his voice out of Heaven to discipline you" (Deuteronomy 4:35 MSG). It goes on to say God personally and powerfully brought you out of Egypt.

We have to go back to the Bible story when the children of Israel were in captivity. Moses asked God, who shall I tell them sent me. God's response was, "I am that I am." Wait. What? Are y'all catching this? God spoke to me and said, "Be still, and know that I am God." He was Moses's I am, and He was mine too. My marriage was symbolic of Egypt because I was held captive by my husband's words over me, keeping my mind and heart in bondage. God heard my cries, and He knew when it was time to step in to lead me to freedom. I'll wait while you have your praise party (for you and me). Go ahead and give it to God!

Listen, there was no way that God would allow me to sit under the oppression of my marriage where my husband would be the only one benefiting from the fallout. Nope. It wasn't going to happen. Everything God showed me was for me to lay down the idol of my marriage and trust in Him. Yes, I had two jokers: my husband and my marriage. OUCH. He showed me that even though I knew about Him, I had not made Him the "I am" of my life. So, what did He do? He stayed faithful to His words when He said He is a consuming firm, a jealous God (Deuteronomy 4:24). In other words, God said, "No, ma'am, I won't have you put anything or anyone before Me. And so that you know that I am God, I will remove it all to discipline you. I want you all to myself, then I'll show you how I restore. It's not about restoring your marriage. I want to restore YOU." Look, He didn't do it to punish me. It was because He loved me so much; He wouldn't have it any other way.

I can say with confidence that all I lost, that was taken away, things I worried about, and the things I tried to hang on to were relinquished and handed over to God. I submitted it to God's will for my life because He knew better than I what this situation would look like in the end. I had to be disciplined and learn under His protecting hand. I had to go through what I did to sincerely know that He is God and has a plan for my life. I couldn't keep running, dodging, or putting it off until I felt safe enough to come out from hiding. God was my safe place, and I had to sit at His feet and get to know Him all over again, but this time for real. I can still hear my best friend Bev telling me, "Chil', sometimes, we're someone else's collateral damage, but God's tool."

God allowed my pain to be the cause for His plan to unfold for me. I didn't know how I was going to get through it. But God saw what I couldn't see. He also reminded me of several occasions when we'd argued about his name not being on the house's deed. Sure, my husband brought the subject up but never made time to make the update because he was too busy on the golf course. Still, he would find some way to turn it back on me. God protected me during those moments because He knew I would have to sell my house later down the road.

It was no different when my husband and I talked about pulling the money out of my 401(k) to purchase a new truck. Each time we discussed it, we'd end up in an argument over something silly. Finally, he told me to forget it because he didn't want my money. Three times God blocked me from giving him the money. He wouldn't let me be a part of his schemes—get this—something I had no idea he was planning. My husband put a plan into motion for my demise. God protected me from my husband and me.

My husband knew the plans he had for building his business. He was adamant about me not coming after his business and made sure I wouldn't get half of it. "Well, thank you, sir, for that gift of greediness you bestowed upon me, geez." God was working each time in His silence back then; so, surely, He'd continue to reveal more.

The entire situation was more than a freakish accident of something falling into my lap. So, I decided to save everything. Every email, every attachment, every fake paystub, and police reports that were part of the fraud were saved to not one, not two, but three hard drives; for safekeeping and a rainy day.

While sitting at the computer I screamed, "Son of a bitch, how could you do this, make me damaged goods to your fraudulent scheme?" Leaning back in the chair, I wanted him to pay for everything he'd put me through. I wanted revenge. I threw everything out the window that I'd been praying for God to do in my marriage. To make matters worse, I thought back to when he didn't sign the "uncontested" divorce papers. It was apparent that God's hand was all over that too because I had no idea what was going on, and Lord knows I wasn't in my right mind.

Because I knew more from his email than I had before, there was nothing left for me to do other than accept things as they were right there in black and white. With all the information I had, answers to some questions, and the big pot of boiling rage, I had a decision to make. I decided I wanted to stick it to him so bad and get everything due to me from this divorce. There was no way he was going to get off easy. I wanted to drag his ass across the hot coals of hell he put me in for no reason. And I was going to use everything in my power and in my hands to make him pay. The important thing to do was hire an attorney who would help me get every penny I deserved from the divorce.

CHAPTER THIRTEEN

My Naked Hand

See if there is any path of pain I'm walking on, and lead me back to your glorious, everlasting ways—the path that brings me back to you. ~ Psalms 139:24 (TPT).

In need of Council

Early February 2019, I decided I needed legal representation with the divorce and researched a few attorneys. I later set up interviews. I decided to press pause with moving forward as it was all too overwhelming. I continued to go back and forth even after all I discovered about him. It seemed like there was one thing after another with this man taking up so much of my life. I did have a life, you know.

In the days following, I made every attempt to keep myself busy with business. As busy as it kept me, the elephant wouldn't leave the room. I couldn't put off retaining an attorney any longer. The longer I waited, the more obsessed I became with checking his emails to see if anything else surfaced. I knew I had no other choice. Within the next week, I decided on who I wanted to handle my case and set up a meeting.

The night before I met the lawyer, I organized the information I'd printed from my husband's emails. I wanted to make sure she had the "big picture" painted for her during our meeting. I must have looked at the papers a hundred times, wondering if I should move forward with changing the filing. I had mixed emotions, but those emotions couldn't squash the most penetrating one of them all; revenge. And just like that, I snapped out of feeling sorry for him and settled on seeing where this would take me and what could be done to make him pay for ruining my life.

The next day, I arrived at the office, and after introductions, I walked her through the steps I'd already taken with filing for an uncontested divorce with the courts. I also discussed what I'd uncovered from the emails and where he stood financially. She asked if I were aware he made that much money. I told her I wasn't, but I knew he had the contract; he just kept the value of it a secret. She went on to question me about the "alleged" emails and the content in them. I could tell she was skeptical as she questioned me, but I knew what I shared with her was the truth. I let her continue to ask questions and saying "alleged." Then she said, "Well, it all comes down to can you prove what you're claiming:" My butt cheeks finally loosened up as I looked her in the eye and said, "Oh, I've got proof for you." That's when I pulled the thick envelope from my lap and slid it across to her.

I sat there quietly as she fingered through the papers. Every minute or so, she would look up at me with a perplexing glance. This went on a few minutes. As she reviewed the paperwork, she looked up at me and said, "You have got to be kidding me. I've seen just about everything in divorce cases, but this is... interesting. How did you pull all of this information together?"

I told her about the invoice showing up in my mailbox, which led me to check his email and how I guessed at passwords and pulled it all together. She said, "Well, you've certainly made things easy to start with, but this could grow legs in many directions, and he could be in a heap of trouble. You do realize that, don't you?" All I could hear inside my head was, *Lady, I don't just want him in a heap of trouble; I want his ass in a whole helluva lot of trouble, and we going big since I can't go back to my "home".* Now, that's what I thought, but I simply responded, "That's on him." She asked if I had taken the information to the police, which I told her I hadn't.

After the formalities were out of the way, and copies were given to her, she happily accepted my case and said, "Thank you for making my job easier." I asked if my husband could foot the bill for my attorney fees. She said he could, and she would make sure of it. I said, "Good, now you're welcome." She advised she would get right on revising the divorce filing, request to have him served papers, and get back in touch later.

As I walked out the door, I released all the breath in my body. I just let it all go. The pressure from that last few months had built up, and I was about to blow. But instead, I just released it, and, somehow, I knew I would be grounded again.

****

As I drew closer to God and looked more to Him for strength and comfort, I often wondered if I'd made the right choice with the divorce. How was it possible to ask God to fix my marriage when my actions were going in a totally different direction. I was more than conflicted. I was in turmoil, confused, and still unsettled with the decision to hire an attorney. I wrestled with how I processed the hurt. I kicked myself in the butt for still feeling love toward my husband. "What in the world are you doing?" I often asked myself. There was no denying I was stuck, full of anxiety, and confused, since I didn't have a choice in the matter of him leaving. I held on to the possibility that God would work it all out for me. Even after deciding to hire an attorney, I continued to go back and forth, questioning if I should go back to the uncontested divorce or stay the course. Either way, I'd still end up divorced.

A few weeks after retaining my lawyer, I was back to being in business mode. But that didn't shake the feelings about my husband. I also made matters worse because I intentionally made it my duty to check his email a few times a week to keep tabs on what he was doing. It became more of a burden than relief because it drew me in further than I anticipated. I figured I would jump in and out without affecting myself, but that wasn't the case. I took one last look into his email to see if anything new happened.

As I finished logging out of his emails, I received a text from him saying his email was being logged into from the area where I lived. I never responded because I cared less about him thinking it was me. Well, when I didn't respond, he called. I answered the phone, and he immediately started cursing, telling me he was taking his computer to the police to report that I hacked into his email and request an investigation. After all his ranting and raving, I said calmly, "Please report me. I'm willing to meet you at the police station. Which one are you going to 'cause I can head out now and be right there? I actually have some information from your email that I need to share as well." There was silence. "Uhhhh, hello? Hello?" It was absolute crickets on the line for a few seconds. "Hey, I really want you to go to the police. Matter of fact, I'm begging you to; so, what's it gonna be"? The next thing I heard was "Click." He hung up, and I didn't hear from him for a while.

It started to weigh me down to the point that I started second-guessing what I had done hiring a lawyer. I still loved him. And as much as he'd hurt me, I didn't feel right trying to hurt him. I was angry with myself for still having those feelings, and if only I had some closure, maybe I wouldn't have felt that way. Plus, I was trying to make sense of the information in his email and why he chose to be deceitful. Inside, I was a ball of mess, and sometimes the ENEMY wasn't my enemy… it was my "inner" me.

Can you imagine loving someone so much that even with the writing on the wall that they no longer love or want you, you still love them? No doubt, at times, I felt I was losing my mind. One day, I hated Reggie and the next, I felt sorry for him, wanting to somehow save him from all the mess. Then soon after, I had thoughts of how much I loved him and wanted him back home where he should have been. I honestly thought my husband was going through a phase or maybe he was having a midlife crisis. I wasn't sure. Despite my emotions, I knew I loved him. I desperately wanted to keep my commitment to Reggie and to God. I was in love. Not only was I in love with my husband, I loved the idea of marriage and being a wife again. Now before you go shaking your head and rolling your eyes at how absurd my thinking was, let me say you're right. But may I also say it's the truth. We can all at least agree that no marriage is perfect. However, the key to a lasting marriage is to put forth the effort to stand when everything around you seems as if it's falling apart. It was no different with my broken marriage, and I wanted Reggie and me to stand together because our marriage was worth the fight. There's no doubt anybody in their right mind would throw down their hands and walk away, leaving the bastard in the dirt. Surely, after all I went through, that should have been my case. But, as I stated from the beginning, I would be honest and share my deepest feelings. I wanted my husband back with me and to live out our vows we made to each other. But I still felt he needed to pay for what he'd done.

My friend Bev told me I was doing more damage to myself going back and forth with my scattered emotions than my husband . I wanted to hate Reggie but couldn't. I had overwhelming concern for him. I grew angrier and angrier that the feelings for him seemed to grow instead of diminishing. I fought emotions to fall back on the divorce and just give him what he wanted. Instead, I decided to keep praying for him and myself as the struggle became more and more intense between love and revenge.

******

The more I struggled with my revenge plot, the more I felt something telling me to leave it alone and let God handle it. I knew my heart wasn't in the right place. I had both hatred and love fighting for the same space (same thing as faith and fear), and I was dying inside. No matter what he'd done, I acted out of character with my plans to pay him back and keeping tabs on him via his email.

At that moment, I was no better than him. My emotions were controlling my every move, and I became toxic. My energy, feelings, mind, and actions were so dark, I hadn't realized I'd fallen back into depression, and there was no way I was going back there. I was spiraling out of control; I couldn't handle this on my own and needed God's help big-time. Sitting at His feet and allowing Him to start the healing was the only thing that could help. I was broken mentally. I was broken physically because I was losing weight. I was spiritually drained because I couldn't hear God's voice with all the junk bottled up inside. And although He was there, I couldn't feel His presence. You're probably questioning what about how He'd revealed my husband's actions, right? I get it. There's no doubt that God's hand was all over it. But that still didn't help me connect with Him on a deeper level because of all the turmoil, which made it difficult for me to lean into Him.

There were occasions I still questioned why He allowed it all and why I had to go through it. Was I sure He had a plan? Yes, but truthfully, I wasn't sure I had enough faith to endure. Emotionally, I was a wreck, as I was crying one day and okay another, and feelings of sadness, depression, and anxiety started all over again.

I needed help. And the only one to help was God. I needed to go to Him for counsel, lay it all at his feet in all sincerity and transparency and not put on a mask of piety and politeness so as not to offend God. No, I would get down and dirty with God so that He could work on my heart and my mind.

I need HIS Counsel

It was late April, a couple months after hiring an attorney. My mind was still in a complete whirlwind about my husband, and I grieved for him after my thoughts settled down a bit from the magnitude of what he had done. My heart ached for him because this was something bigger than I could ever imagine in my gut. And I didn't know what it was. So, what did I do? I started praying for my husband and asked God to cover him and shield him from the impact of his actions, whatever the outcome. But what I really desired was for him to become aware of what he was doing and how wrong it was before he went too far. I couldn't rest knowing he was capable of doing the things I saw in the email. I was in complete disbelief and wanted my husband to feel sorry for what he had done. But strangely enough, I doubted he even cared. There was a part of me in disbelief about everything he'd done, and I felt sorry for him. I loved him and didn't want anything harmful to happen to him. There was a possibility he could serve time in prison if found out, and I didn't want that, no matter how much anger and disgust I felt.

In addition to feeling sorry for him, I blamed myself for not seeing the signs and getting out of the marriage earlier. I questioned why I married him and why I still cared for him when God showed his hand and HIS too. I knew God would be the only one to hold me up during the days ahead. I couldn't stop thinking of him, and although I was too pissed at him, I had a heart of compassion for him as well. It didn't matter what he'd done; he was still a person that God loved. And we've all done outlandish things we wouldn't want anyone to know about. Despite it all, I got to see a decent side of him when we were together. He had a tender side at times. He was as comical as they'd come, and he always spoke of helping others from his hometown when he "made it big," so to speak. These were a few of the things that made it easy to love him. But he got caught up in pride, greed, and a false narrative he created about doing good no matter its cost.

All of it was too much for me to handle. I didn't understand why I put the weight of his actions on me because all it did was make me suffer from the impact of the feelings and emotional roller coaster ride, and I couldn't get off. Moreover, I was upset with myself that I cared so much about what would happen to him, but he needed to be confronted somehow in the same vein. Then there was me wallowing over my divorce. Not really wanting a divorce, but I knew that's where my marriage was headed. So, maybe I should give it one more try. Maybe I should reach out to him and ask him to go away with me to just talk one last time.

The excitement filled me, and without even thinking, I picked up the phone to call him. As the phone rang, I told myself he wouldn't answer, but he did. I played around with the niceties for a brief moment, and then I went for the juggler. I put it all out there and told him of my plans to take a trip to the resort property we had and asked if he would come with me, just one last time to talk. There was a brief hesitation from him, then he said that wouldn't be a good idea because a family member passed away, and he'd be out of town.

The conversation ended on a decent note, and I'd done what I set out to accomplish, inviting him. Although it was sure to fail, I felt the need for me to go alone. I needed some time to "be still" and lean into God.

The Resort Reset

I decided to book the trip to San Antonio. I needed to seek God's will for my debacle of a life. And as God would have it, I felt a nudge that wouldn't quit for the next few days. Oddly enough, it was more about me than "him."

Driving to the resort, a surge of tears welled up inside of me as I drove along the highway. It was my desire to meet with God, along with everything that pressed on my heart and mind. I truly needed a release. As I continued along, I put on some music and praised my way to the resort. When I arrived and went to my room, I realized I didn't have a plan. So, I set my bags down and began pacing around the room. I remember asking God, "Well, what are we going to do now that I'm here? I need answers, and I need them now—how I see myself, how I see you, and how you see me. God, I need answers about my marriage, my businesses, my family, and my finances. So, God, that's what I want to talk to you about while I'm here." Yep, I know it seemed like a lot to ask of God, but when your life has been turned upside down, inside out, and nothing working in your favor, you too will need answers.

As I pondered my intentions, I sat down in a chair and settled in to hear God's voice. In my mind, I heard, "Routine Christian." I sat quietly, listening inwardly, and thought about my routine. It was clear that I went through the motions of daily devotions or weekly church attendance just so those activities could be checked off my "being with Jesus" list. I felt ashamed knowing there were times I didn't remember what I read in my devotions or heard after Sunday service. Sometimes, I remembered, maybe, but most times, no. I almost didn't want to believe it, and I certainly didn't want my time with God to be shallow.

Guilt overcame me when I realized that wasn't the relationship I wanted with God. I never thought I had a checklist relationship, but it was true. I "worked" for my relationship with God. God showed me that I was going through the mechanics of religion, the motions, and all the false pretenses of my relationship with Him. I felt pitiful, but I at, least, came to grips with my reality. So, I emptied my heart to Him, accepted the truth, and asked for forgiveness. But I couldn't stop there. I needed Him to show me what it was to know Him.

Hours had passed as I sat ashamed but free from performing for God. I was ready to start my discovery of why I was there. What did I want and need from God? Now mind you, I've asked Him these questions many times at different intervals in my life. Then, I looked at the room desk. I saw all my journals and reading material I'd brought with me to "draw closer" to God. At least six of them I'd used in the past. What a mess! I had all that stuff I'd written about, happenings over my life, and things I recognized I needed to change. But the results were no different. Looking at that pile of journals told me I was all over the place, and it had to stop.

As I looked at the heap of materials, I grabbed a pamphlet my mom had given to me a couple of months earlier. I picked it up and started reading it, and the words seemed as if they were jumping off the page. They resonated immediately with my situation.

I began reading about trials we go through and how they're all part of God's will for our lives. As I read more, I realized God was trying to teach me how to deal with adversity (husband leaving) before His deliverance. Right there, it talked about love, trust, patience, how to give thanks in every situation, and especially, stop concentrating on what happened and thank Him that He was in charge of what was happening. I was undergoing spiritual development, and I was fighting hard against what God was trying to do. I didn't realize it until that moment. God knew what direction my life was headed. Indeed, I would be able to see His provisions for me when I got out of His way. Every attempt I made at resisting what He was doing resulted in more damage to myself because I was in the way of receiving what God promised me. He told me to be still, and I did everything else but what He said. I was more concerned with managing the situation myself. Then, God reminded me to remember when He brought me out of past situations. There wouldn't be a reason to doubt if He can do again when I find myself in something that seems impossible. For me, that is.

That was the beginning of what I could expect God to do and say to me. I reconciled that I wanted to control things, and that wouldn't work any longer. Obviously, I hadn't heeded His earlier warning of repent, yield, and get myself out the way.

******

The next morning began with heaviness, and I wasn't about to do devotion after yesterday. My mind was already on my husband and everything he'd done. My emotions ranged from anger, embarrassment, frustration, played like a fool, betrayal, pissed, revenge, hatred, and, wouldn't you know it, love. But, despite my many emotions, I too had a part in the marriage breaking down. If I were to get past the emotions, I had to take responsibility as well.

I knew I had to go back to the beginning. I needed God's strength to walk me through the relationship from the beginning to show me the truth about my part. Knowing it would make me feel horrible, it was time to face yet another truth about the signs I missed. Or should I say overlooked?

That visit to the past didn't take 10 mins to trace back the signs in our relationship. My mind was on rewind times 10, and like a flash of light, I saw the signs were present, but I ignored them. I had overlooked eleven significant signs, and I dare not list them here. Just know they all fell into the categories of money, respect, love, or the lack of them. I suffered from emotional and mental abuse from my husband as he failed to make me a priority. What an eye-opener.

Going back down memory lane helped me see how much my husband sought to get everything he wanted and needed from me as a wife but wouldn't love me or anything else that came with loving me. I wasn't a perfect wife, but I was a great wife to him. I never disrespected him. I made our house a home, handled the bills, and made sure he had a soft place to land when he came home from work. I wanted to love on him, spend quality time, worship together, and more. But what ended up happening was me losing myself and God as well. My marriage became an idol. I gave away my personality just to keep him happy. Turning the focus toward me, I had some soul searching to do. I also needed to learn the lessons and determine where I was headed next.

Let me stick a pin right here and say that when you genuinely do some serious and intentional self-assessing, God won't take long to reveal the truth to you. Being honest with God and wanting to know how I'd gotten off course and how tight my mask was on, it didn't take long for me to resolve that I tend to control the outcome of situations and manipulate people for things to go in my favor. Ouch! I gave more of myself when I really didn't want to give anything, which left me feeling depleted and agitated. Ouch again. I overlooked negative behavior when it should have been addressed. I didn't put myself first, say no, and stand up for what I wanted or needed. Geez! Bottom line, I gave a damn too much. "Now, we're getting somewhere, Rhlonda!" As if that weren't enough, I lived my life by helping others accomplished their goals and invested in their lives more than my own.

To put it frankly, I was an imposter. I came across as if I had it all together, but I really didn't. Most of what I did was to get "Atta-girl" from others. Deep inside, the real me was masked. Even though I was successful by the world's standards, I failed miserably by God's standards. I didn't see myself the way God did, and that was the most awful realization by far. Looking at my situation from both sides, I had to point a finger in my direction, not just my husband's. He did what I allowed him to get away with doing to me, point-blank. As for me, well, I was smack dab in the middle of an identity crisis, my view vs. God's view. I poured my heart out to God for help. I was in desperate need of a makeover on the inside.

I was reeling from hurt and disappointment. Although I told God I wanted my marriage, at that point, I was more interested in what He wanted for my life. I couldn't try to control the outcome any longer. I wanted to believe God fully for whatever He had in mind when He whispered for me to "be still." All that was left was to trust Him and give everything to Him. No matter how it turned out, it would be for my good.

******

My life was no surprise to God. Shocker, right? He knew every turn I would make. He had an appointment with me in that season, which He scheduled a long time before it showed up on my timetable. So, I knew He would take care of me and give me the strength to go forward in Him. God loved me. But most of all, He wanted me to love me too.

Afterward, I felt refreshed. Although I had to accept the truth about myself, I also had to adopt new ways of thinking and different approaches to handling things when life happened. So, I decided to get real and accept that I was (and still am) a broken woman who's loved by God. All I can do is continually seek out the truth and readily accepts my flaws. I love that I have a big heart, but I understand that it requires me to set boundaries, so I won't have to continually be in protective mode. I decided to live at peace with myself, all while trusting God's will for my life and His definition of me according to His word; nobody else. I would no longer accept lies, noncommitment, or betrayal. Putting myself first, respecting, and loving myself would be the guiding force behind all that I'd do. My day had been filled with releasing, reflecting, revising, and refocusing. With very little energy left, I felt great. I no longer had a heaviness about my marriage. I'd done my part, and now it was up to God to walk me through the rest.

On the last day during my "resort restoration," early that morning, I woke up and reflected on the last two days. The plan I had in my mind looked nothing like what took place. I thought I would spend that time praying over every area of my life, but those two days were spent primarily on my marriage and a long look at myself. Although some thoughts were still toward my husband, I had a better perspective of my control issues and accepted what would become of my relationship with my husband. God did what He had planned for me to do and not what I planned. But He was so gracious to let me participate.

The Pattern

Upon returning home from the resort, I recognized a pattern as I read through the gazillion journal notes. The pattern was "I." The focus of my questions was toward me, and the pattern was control and trust. Still? Funny enough, I thought I had this under control, but it was evident I'd been in the same place, talking about the same two things, for a very long time. Then it hit me (thank you, Holy Spirit); my thoughts were centered around me. How can "I "do this, or how can "I "change that. When I say "I," it takes God entirely out of the picture and places the reigns of my life in my hands. It kept me from surrendering control to God because I put myself before Him. Bottom line, I'd been asking all the wrong questions, which didn't change my situation. I also thought I was in lockstep with God, only to realize I was full of pride, thinking I had the answers and had it all figured out. My spiritual insight was running on empty or near empty. I thought I could do my life, in my strength, and in my way.

God revealed this to remind me to surrender everything over to Him, including my marriage. What I loved most about it was He knew when to reveal it to me. His timing was impeccable.

There was no way I would have seen myself or accepted myself with a warped understanding. He was getting me ready throughout the entire separation and isolation He had me in. First, I had to come to the realization and truth about my control issues. Secondly, God showed my heart to me the way He saw it. The controlling and distrusting person I operated as wasn't how He saw me. Lastly, submitting to God's will would begin when I released control of the outcome to Him. He knew when I'd be open to receive it, and, that day, I most certainly did.

Now, I'm not saying, "Snap, I'm healed," but, at least, now, when I recognize my controlling actions, I can submit to God, resist the temptation to try to control things, and give it back to God.

But that wouldn't be the last of my heart being exposed. That was the beginning of God showing me things about myself that I never dared to see in myself before. "Before I formed you in the womb I knew you, before you were born I set you apart; I appointed you..." (Jeremiah 1:5)

The New Naked

In light of taking accountability for my actions, owning my mistakes, and getting a good ol' whooping from God, I was desperate for my life to be different in how I saw myself, others, and, especially, God. I realized my self-image was damaged to the point of not trusting in myself or God, and I'm not about to talk about not loving myself. I knew I loved God in my own way of understanding, but that needed repairing too.

All that God showed me during my separation and, ultimately, divorce pointed to trust and love. God was pressing upon my heart, "Can you love Me with all your heart and trust Me when you can't trace Me? Will you trust Me when you can't hear Me clearly? Will you be still long enough for Me to change you into Christlikeness?" These questions burned within me as if He were sitting right next to me talking. I could feel His presence connect with me intimately like never before. I knew for me to do that, I had to open up, and I mean all the way up like bare-boned naked before Him.

Thinking of baring all before God, as if He didn't already know, didn't feel strange to me. But no one taught me how to be "that" bold. Then I thought about how my best friend Bev and I talked with one another. I thought, *Chil', you're going a little too far thinking you can say all of that to God.* Then I laughed a really good belly laugh that I hadn't had in months. Certainly, I sounded foolish and thought, God already heard us talking before, so how was I gonna hold back from Him what I don't from her? What, He can't handle it, but she can?"

Was I being a phony with God? It's not that I didn't "know" because I did. I've had deep conversations about God and all that He is and how He can do anything, yada, yada, yah. BUT… I never applied it to me. I encouraged others and there I was in despair and gutted. Just wide open exposed, and I had to sit there. Unable to move at the revelation of it all, God was clearly asking me, "Are you willing to lay down all the false perceptions about you and Me that you've been holding on to and let Me give you a fresh revelation of who I am and who you are"?

As I sat there, I wanted more of Him. The refreshing of His lingering presence was definitely what I needed. So, I leaned in and let the emotions go; I sobbed. I snuggled up into my father's hand and let Him begin the healing process. And what a process it would be. I needed healing from every lie the enemy tried to speak over my life, emotional healing, spiritual healing (sorry Marvin Gaye, I don't need that kind of healing), self-image healing, and all the other healings I hadn't faced. Look, let's all agree I needed surgery, okay?

God knew how I'd been living, thinking, and seeing things that needed to be dismantled or should I say surgically removed. He ushered me into surgery after my marriage broke down because my heart was out of rhythm. My marriage had an irregular heartbeat, up and down, and skipping all over the place. As a matter of fact, it seemed as if it had stopped beating altogether, and I was numb. If He didn't do something soon, I would die (inside).

God couldn't bless me the way He wanted to if I couldn't be authentic. God was telling me I had to get real. Not with Him but with myself because He already knew who I was. I was the one who lost the memo. He couldn't get His character to shine through me if I continued to hide and put on façades. God spoke intimately to me and said, "I know this is how YOU see yourself, and dear, you've been misinformed for a long time now. That's NOT how I made you, and it's not how I see you. Until you stop going against the grain of what I'm trying to accomplish and allow Me to remove spiritual cataracts from your eyes, you'll continue with a warped image that's false and hide the true identity of My daughter, who I created and love. And make no mistakes about it; I don't make mistakes. Neither do I lie or change My mind. I say who you are because I know who I am. You say who you are because you don't know Me like you think you do. So, what's it gonna be?"

I was almost offended. God just went off on me. And for the shade of it all, the only thing I could do was lean back and say, "Daaaang, Lord." Of course, I couldn't deny one word of what I'd heard. Here's the funny part, the way He slayed me is the same way I would have given it to someone else. So, I know it was nobody but God speaking my language, "the way He made me." And He did it in such a lovingly, sarcastic, heartfelt, beat yo' head till the while meat show kinda way. Ya know what I mean. I felt everything He shared with me as I sat in stillness. But His righteous right hand was holding me up. I was safe and secure in His loving hand.

In contemplation of all that God was doing, my mind shifted to Reggie. The divorce was in limbo and that was my chance to wash my hands of my husband. I had a nagging feeling to let it all go: Reggie and the divorce. I couldn't control it any longer nor did I want to. I knew I had to go back to the original agreement of the divorce after my encounter with God. Knowing I would walk away with little to nothing, and after everything I'd already loss in the process, I also came to the conclusion I didn't want anything from him or his business because it was connected to the fraud he committed. It was "dirty" money, and I didn't want to be associated with it. I called Reggie, and, to my surprise, he answered the phone. I told him I no longer wanted to fight with him over the divorce and that I was done trying to reason with him to come back. I told him I was thinking of reversing the contested divorce but only if he agreed to give me $50K and pay for all my attorney fees. Initially, he went off, cursing, telling me he wasn't going to give me another penny other than what we agreed. During his rampage, I sat in silence. Little did he know, I was praying, asking God to give me the strength to say the right thing without losing it and spilling the beans about the fraud he committed. Finally, I asked, "Are you done because in order for me to go back to uncontested status, you will give me what I just asked, or we can fight this all the way to the bank." I don't know what it was about what I said, but, for the first time, Reggie heard me. He agreed to the revision. I told him I'd let my attorney know to revise the papers and hung up.

After hanging up, I had a sense of relief. I felt as if the dark cloud over my head was lifted. Let me be clear, I still wanted him to pay for wrecking my life. I even imagined Reggie had the biggest smile on his face, gloating over the fact that he'd won again. But this time, I chuckled and thought of what Joseph said to his brothers who betrayed him in Genesis 50:20. Allow me to paraphrase, "Reggie, your evil will be for my good; you just wait and see." At that point, it was no longer my issue. I decided to let God be God for now. I contacted my attorney to let her know of my decision to revert to the uncontested divorce but, this time, with $50K and all attorney fees owed to him. She questioned if I were certain, given everything I'd shared with her. I told her I was confident that I was making the right choice.

After hanging up with my attorney, as I sat on the couch, everything I had gone through for the last few months raced through my mind like lightening. And just like that, I had resolved to let it go and Reggie too. No more fighting. No more attorneys to fight our battles. No court appearance to plead my case to the judge. It would soon be all over, and Reggie could move on and I could start over. Sounds good right? You may think so, but the battle was not over, just yet.

CHAPTER FOURTEEN

His Loving Hand

When you pass through the waters, I will be with you; and when you pass through the rivers, they will not sweep over you. When you walk through the fire, you will not be burned; the flames will not set you ablaze.
~ Isaiah 43:2.

God was silent still as I was waited on the attorneys to move the case forward. As a matter of fact, there was no activity for three months. As thoughts of my pending divorce crossed my mind, I heard a question deep within my heart. What should I be doing while I wait? Sure, I was busy working on both businesses, trying to find work, but even that was a struggle. My consulting firm was at a standstill, and the brokerage was, well, just there. So, I waited.

The weekend before my business trip was difficult. I felt a heaviness on me that I couldn't shake. Early in the morning, as I walked around the house, I started thinking about God's timing for the divorce and waiting through the silence. It seemed as if I had waited for so long to hear from the attorneys, and zero, zilch, nada was all I was left with in anticipation to hear something. I ain't going to lie; I thought since nothing was happening, God was surely preparing my husband and me to reunite. At least I'd hoped on the possibility. For some strange reason I thought it could happen. But who was I fooling? I felt the heaviness as if the atmosphere were shifting and the sky was about to fall. So, whatever He was doing, I knew He was preparing me, so I continued to pray.

My thoughts shifted to my husband with an urge to call him. It was a few days before his birthday, and I felt rather sad. I wouldn't spend it with him. Then the feelings grew intense. I thought of driving to his apartment. What a crazy thought, but I went with it. At first, I went back-and-forth until I found myself in the car, headed his way. I prayed for the right words to say, still not wanting to nag or tick him off. Then I heard, "You gotta tell him." Say what? Naw, that couldn't be what the bubble-gut feeling I had was. But there was no denying it. Everything in me was screaming for me to tell him everything I knew. *But why now?* I thought. I didn't think that would salvage the relationship. Nevertheless, I had some email spying to confess to. My gut was telling me to come clean. Or perhaps it was the weight of the guilt I carried for so long.

My stomach was in a knot the entire ride. The one thing I knew was I didn't want to keep living with this "secret" of what I'd done to him, all while accusing him of what he'd done to me. I'm not saying that his and my actions were on the same level, but hell, a white lie is still a lie. It was the same hypocritical nonsense I was engrossed in charging him with, and I wanted it off my conscious. Call me what you want, but you won't call me "Guilty Gertrude." Nope, not gonna happen. I was about to tell him everything. And above that, if he knew that I knew, then he couldn't say I didn't tell him before everything came crashing down around him. Right? Exactly.

When I arrived at the apartment, his car wasn't there, so I called him. After he answered, I told him I wanted to be honest about something, and I needed him to be honest with me. I told him about the emails, everything I saw, everything he did when he left, and how it made me feel. I went on and on about the lies he tried to make me believe, forcing my hand to file the divorce; I mean, I went in hot. I told him I was done, but I needed him to know that he only got by but didn't get away with anything. During my "emptying," he said nothing. Not. A. Word. Now, I'll go out on a limb and say it was because he didn't know if I was recording the call (which I wasn't). He was either smart or paranoid enough not to respond in any way, and his reaction was one that I expected. I knew he wouldn't show his hand, so his silence told me everything I needed to know.

The conversation shifted to the marriage (probably by me), where he continued to blame me for the relationship breaking down. He was good at deflecting because it was the only defense he knew. He most certainly wouldn't take accountability for anything he'd done. He stated we were too far gone, and he still wanted the divorce. That's when I reminded him we hadn't heard from our lawyers. "Hey, why don't we pray and ask God what we should do. Will you pray with me?" Then he said, yep, I can do that with you." Whaaaat! He agreed? Now, I've asked him to pray with me many times before, and the answer was always no, but this time, he said yes without hesitation.

I asked him to lead the prayer, but I think I took the request a little too far because he declined. So as the wife who always prayed for her husband, I began to pray. First, I thanked God that he agreed to pray with me. Then, I asked God to show us where this marriage stood if we were to stay in the marriage or not and to make the answer so straightforward that we'd know it was from God. We both said, "Amen." Then I said, "God, by the way, show us this week, Amen." Reggie asked why I said this week. I told him that we needed to ask Him for something specific for us to know that it was from God. After praying and some brief niceties that were exchanged, we hung up. I felt so good because I just knew, I knew God would answer that prayer. I didn't care about the silence from the attorneys, and I didn't care about the divorce. I felt the spirit of acceptance come over me, and all was peaceful.

A few days later, I was in San Francisco on business. It was also my husband's birthday. I texted him happy birthday that morning and went straight to work. I was so busy, there was no time to check my email. Later that afternoon, when things slowed down, I decided to check my email, and I sat there dumbfounded with the wind knocked out of me.

My final divorce papers were sitting at the very top of my email list. I could hardly breathe, nor could I believe it. You mean to tell me after all this time I prayed and asked God to save my marriage, and the one time we prayed together as husband and wife was the prayer God answered? So many emotions rushed over me, but God answered our prayer. Humph, what a nice gift he got that year for his birthday.

It was time to do what I had been dreading for the last nine months; sign the divorce papers. I sat there looking at the email string, and there were two times the lawyers communicated before April and absolutely none from May 2 through June 3. Well, nothing that is until we prayed together but too little too late. If God answered our prayer as husband and wife on that request, just think of what He could have done in our marriage had we prayed together before he walked out. I know the power of prayer and all its possibilities, but, unfortunately, I didn't experience it so much in my marriage.

Still in shock about the divorce, I closed the email and went back to work. My peer and I went out for dinner and drinks after work. She could tell there was something weighing on my mind, so I shared with her that I'd gotten the divorce papers and how I was feeling. To my surprise, I didn't fall to pieces emotionally. The dark cloud had been lifted, and I wholeheartedly accepted the fact my divorce was final and my marriage over. At that moment, I did the "oh well" shoulder shrug, pulled my chin up, and did a mic drop on trying to maintain control. The time had come to move on. But I knew it wouldn't be easy.

After returning from my business trip, I leaned into God more than ever. I still needed His strength to get me past my divorce. As I drew closer to him, my heart ached more and more, or perhaps there was a longing. This time, it was toward God. I just couldn't get enough of Him. I started spending more time with him and speaking His word into my life. But I felt I was just going through the motions again. Yes, I wrestled with letting go of the hurt, getting past the betrayal, and the lingering anger, and quite honestly, "speaking life" just wasn't cutting it. My heart was experiencing a different level of hurt and tugging. I started feeling sorry for myself. I grieved me, and it was a heaviness I couldn't describe. I felt sorry for myself because of the darkness I had in my heart. Oh God, another cleansing. What more was there to empty out? And why did it have to come back to back? The emotional instability was really pissing me off, and I wanted it to be over. Whatever the truth was, I beaconed God to give it to me straight. Enough was enough.

Heart Issues

A short time after the divorce, I was back in the groove of working my business. It was a pleasant surprise that the depression seemed to be lifted. I looked toward a new life, and peace of mind was starting to settle in. Of course, I thought of my ex-husband, probably more than I should, but I wasn't going to fake my feelings as if I had none. It would take some time getting over him, and I understood it would be a process. I even told myself there would be some days it would hit me more than others and to acknowledge those feeling and release them quickly. The first couple of times it happened, I was successful. Little did I know I still had some unresolved issues to deal with.

Lying in bed, with my thoughts all over the place, it sank in that my divorce was signed and the ink had dried. My marriage and "Mrs. Washington" were no more. The tears came out of nowhere and I bawled my eyes out, thinking I couldn't handle being divorced. Feelings of frustration rose within as I told God I needed him to help me.

Now, mind you, God still wasn't speaking, but I felt a sense of comfort over me. With my eyes closed, I yearned to feel His presence more, and that's when I got a blurry vision of a throne with me walking toward it. I saw someone who sat on one side, and beside me walking, there was someone else. The image of me walking toward the massive throne was majestic. I felt a warm and peaceful awareness all around me and tried to jolt myself back to reality. I knew it wasn't a dream because I wasn't sleeping. It was God's presence, and Jesus was escorting me to the throne of God.

Suddenly, I freaked out because it was so real. I thought for a split second I was dead but slowly calmed down as the energy around me was loving and peaceful. Tears began to fall down my face. I was in awe that God was right there with me. I had the firsthand experience of being wrapped in God's presence. My heart was beating fast, and I could barely catch my breath. But there was a rhythm to it, and I felt at peace at the same time.

At that moment, I knew this was my chance to tell God everything. I sobbed like a baby, telling Him that I needed Him. I said, "God, I'm tired. I'm tired." I must have said it a hundred times when my spirit led me to "You will seek Me and find Me when you seek Me with all of your heart." Hearing this, I jumped straight up out of the prayer and grabbed my Bible to search for the scripture. I knew this one, and for a few minutes, I searched. You know how it is when you know something for sure, and you just can't seem to pull it together. I was way over in Deuteronomy. As frustrated as I was, I kept looking because I knew that it had to be God. I was already struggling with God being silent and heard it in my spirit as clear as my own momma's voice. I was determined to find the scripture if it took all night. I was at my wit's end, nervous and excited at the same time. Chil', I put that paper Bible down and picked up the phone to use the Bible app. I rolled my eyes so hard when it pulled up Jeremiah 29:3. Well, I sought that scripture with all my heart and finally found it. It was just what I needed.

Rocking back and forth in the bed, I kept repeating the verse in my mind. Then it got shorter to... "Seek me with your whole heart." As I focused on that phrase for a few minutes, it became shorter to simply "whole heart... your whole heart, Rhlonda, your whole heart." I sat there, pondering over what was in my heart. What kept me from hearing and finding God the way I longed for Him? So, I stayed right there. "God, help me. I want to know what's in my heart that's keeping me from You." No sooner than it fell from my lips, I saw the word "fear" flash in my mind, which was no surprise. Now I'm mad at myself because I had been over this my entire life, and it was still there. No way, I wasn't going to have it any longer. I told God I was ready to be honest with Him about what was in my heart, and didn't care what He revealed to me. Something was jumping in my spirit; there was probably more.

By this time, I'm repeating the word "fear." What was I afraid of and why? As I continued to pray, I got candid with myself and admitted I was fearful of not being good enough. I also admitted my fear of being rejected and lonely. Somehow, thoughts of being incapable of taking care of myself, like I had before, crept into my mind. I confessed my fears of the business failing, not being loved, not having any money, not being accepted. I sobbed that nothing was working out for me (like I wanted it to), especially not knowing my life's purpose and fear of being stuck.

I'll be honest and admit I was more fearful of my purpose because I had a full career with all the things that I'd accomplished prior. But now I had a half-baked business and my life was on pause. I questioned what God was calling me to at this age. I yelled out in frustration, "I'm 49, on the verge of 50, and ain't nobody got time to start over. I'm too old for this stuff, I pleaded my case to God. Then I realized Chil' I sounded like Sarah when she laughed. But it was frightening for me, you know, the "not knowing". The list was long, and I didn't realize how deep fear kept me from God.

Years ago, in His infinite wisdom, God showed me I had a warped perspective of who He is. I remember taking a sabbatical from church and all the religious exercises because my spirit was tired. I was tired of "working" to get God's approval. I wanted to know God more personally, and I knew I couldn't do that in church. Well, it was one of the best experiences I'd had as I came to truly understand that if God is anything, He is love. He is full of love, patience, and kindness toward us, no matter how many times we fail. He patiently waits for us to surrender our pride, strength, knowledge (which I call my god complex) of how things should be, and takes each of the details in our life and use it for our good. I'm here to remind you, God's nurturing love is tender and gentle. He is slow to get angry yet swift to show us His faithful love (Psalms 86:15-TPT). But, somewhere along the way, in all my doing and proving, I'd forgotten what He showed me back then and fell back into religious exercises.

At that moment, sitting in the bed, God showed me that fear kept me from fully trusting in Him. I paid lip service to Him regarding trust, but my heart, well, that was another thing. Fear made me doubt everything about myself. I focused on what was next in my life without dealing with what was happening in that present moment. God basically stripped me naked (again) but did it in such a loving way that He showed me more of myself without judgment. His hand was on my heart as He began to massage and loosen the fear and doubt buried deep within.

That experience with God was the most freeing moment I'd ever had. Throughout the entire process, God helped me see it wasn't about my ex-husband or the marriage anymore. He showed me that because fear filled me, I tried to manipulate the outcome of situations. I had malice, hatred, unforgiveness, deceit, rage, enviousness, and everything else in my heart. And because of that clutter, there was no place for His spirit to reside freely. Talk about not knowing yourself. I asked myself, "Girl, who are you?" Because she wasn't who I wanted to be. I needed to release that mess, and I wanted it right at that moment. I asked God to forgive me simplistic and sure, without a doubt.

As I laid there exhausted, I began thanking Him. Then I heard Him say, "That's why you're controlling because you fear." My head sprang off the pillow because I knew, without a shadow of a doubt, I heard His voice. Finally, finally! I heard from God. So much joy came over me that I laughed and cried at the same time.

Nevertheless, He chided me about my control issues, which was quite funny 'cause I heard it in a familiar and sarcastic voice. But it didn't matter. I accepted the truth because not only did He hear and answer me, I heard Him. In the silence, He showed me how much He loves me because He gave me what He knew I could receive. And, I love Him for patiently waiting for the perfect time.

For the Fraud of It

After my encounter with God, I committed to sitting in His presence to allow Him to massage my heart. Trust me, this wasn't an overnight quick fix because there was so much damage to be repaired from what had consumed me. I was in the process of detoxing from lousy doctrine, evil thoughts, deadly speech, and destructive emotional behaviors.

Even though months had passed since I discovered the fraud, every now and then, it crossed my mind, and I was infuriated at just the thought of what he'd done. Although I didn't have access to his emails anymore, I couldn't help but think that he was living life to the fullest while I yet struggled. I thought I'd get past the bitterness and rage, but I hadn't because I hadn't seen any results of his wrongdoing or better yet, arrest. Good Lord, did I want the man arrested? I wasn't sure, but I wanted him to pay for all the hurt he caused me.

Even after God exposed what was in my heart, and I was spending more time with Him, at times, I poached the idea of whether or not to report him. I mean, c'mon, there was no way he should get away with fraud, stealing, lying, and cheating. Nope huh-uh, mostly since I was the fallout of his premeditated fraud. No way! I had to do something. I even went so far as to use David's plea for my own defense when he said, "So now, O Lord, don't forget about me. Take note of how I have been humiliated at the hands of those or *"him" (emphasis added)* who hate me" (Psalm 9:13 TPT). I wanted the worst revenge possible for him. I wanted to be the one to expose him so he could feel a small portion of the pain he caused me.

The bitterness simmered in my heart as I continued to wrestle with trying to justify the reason for "doing the right thing." I knew full well the underlying reason was that I still experienced the aftershocks of hurt and betrayal at his hands. Of course, I realized I was being the judge, jury, and prosecutor instead of allowing God to "chisel" my ex-husbands heart like He said he would. But even that wouldn't be enough to concede. Instead, I convinced myself and told God that it was the right thing for me to do.

Quite honestly, my aim of revenge towards Reggie was because my marriage didn't turn out the way I wanted it to after going into the relationship with nothing but the best of intentions of being committed to him. And if you really wanna know the truth behind my revenge, it boils down to three things. Number one, for the first time in my life, I knew that being a good wife was being a companion and a partner. I had to change so many things about myself, and I worked on those things to be a good wife to Reggie. I worked on my mouth, my words and how I spoke to him, and even the way I would respond to him. I worked on my attitude and how I could be better in support of my husband because that's what I was called to be. I tried my damnedest, and that moves me to reason number two. In my trying, I suggested that we go to counseling. I tried talking to him numerous times, and every time we tried to have a conversation about what was on my heart, I invited him into that space in hopes that he would connect to me and see my truest intensions. I invited him to attend church like we did when we dated. I asked him to pray with me and for us to worship together. Hell, I wanted us to read scripture together and for him to cover me in prayer. I included him in everything every step of the way. I supported him in everything and the entire time I expressed my concerns to him, I still felt like I had no voice. Lastly, after all was said and done, after all my attempts and investments into our marriage, he still left. I knew then that the real reason he left had nothing to do with me. He knew I wouldn't be part of his scheme, and he had no problem with conjuring up some wild notion that I was the reason for the marriage breaking down. And, when he left, he left me with nothing. There was nothing within me, nothing in my mind, nothing in my bank account, nothing I could count on. I couldn't lean on anything because I spent so much time pouring it all into my marriage and him. Yep, I said it because that's what happened. He upgraded when we got together. And after all that, I was pissed. That's why I wanted revenge.

Therefore, after much contemplation, going back and forth on what to do, I decided to report him to the company he contracted with and watch everything he had crash and burn. I retrieved one of the thumb drives I'd saved for a rainy day. And baby, that day, it was storming. I organized everything chronologically and categorized all the documents. As I read through each one, I highlighted pertinent information, labeled them as exhibits, and crafted a detailed explanation for the documents. I treated this case as one of my past high-profile investigations and gave it the special attention it deserved. I was all in on this one because I had nothing to lose.

I called the company's fraud division to get their lead investigator's contact information. Set on revenge, I would finally get justice when they caught him. Listen, this was no petty crime. He manufactured fake documents, people, and signatures to get paid off the invoices he submitted. The bottom line is he left me so that he could steal. Are you kidding me? I'm snitching period! So, I gathered the information, called the investigator and shared all the details I had with him. I told him I'd mail him everything I had, which I did. I finally pulled the trigger, but that's when the wrestling started.

The Invisible Intervention

Days after I had spoken with the investigator, I was very uneasy. Reporting Reggie's fraud felt as if I betrayed him. Go figure. I remember lying in the bed one night praying, and I asked God to forgive me for taking matters into my own hands again. Overwhelming guilt came over me, and I broke down. I was sick about what I had done. C'mon, I'm being honest so don't judge me. I cried out and asked God to forgive me. Hell, I even prayed that God would give Reggie the strength to endure whatever would come of me reporting him.

I didn't hear back from the investigator for a month or so, then one day, I got a call. He told me after everything had been reviewed, although some things were in question, they couldn't confirm the fraud, and they were closing the case. He went on to say that he'd keep my information if anything came up in the future.

After hanging up, I felt a sense of relief but also shock. I couldn't believe it, knowing what I found in his email. Even when I spoke with my Reggie, he knew I had information on his fraudulent activities and probably thought I could report him.

"Now what, Rhlonda? Your bright idea didn't work," I told myself. Look, I knew I was taking matters into my own hands, acting on revenge, and in place of God. But nothing came of it that day. I told God I was falling back, washed my hands of it, and thought of it less often as before.

I was relieved that God intervened and saved me from myself once again. I had that thing in motion, and God stayed my hand and basically said, "Not so fast, not now." I thought about all the massaging God had done on my heart, the progress I'd made, and all the times God showed me His hand. And I had the gall to go off on my own? Ha! He shut it all the way down.

I believe God intervened in my plot for revenge to remove what wasn't like Him and to make room for what He had for me. God saw me on a path that He knew would set me back from the progress I had made depending on Him. If I would have stayed on that course, I would have become a burden to it. So, He took the weight of my plot off me by allowing the case to be inconclusive. And then He carried the weight of the impact of my guilt because He cared so much for me. Taking matters into my own hands to report Reggie wasn't my call and I was out of line. Or should I say out of His will. I concluded that when I reported him, it would bring me some sort of satisfaction for Reggie's betrayal, walking out, and not sticking to his promise. That's what I was most angry about; he didn't keep his promise to love me. But God revealed to me that my plan of revenge was basically me telling God that I could do it better than He could, and mine had to do with punishment, while His had everything to do with bringing Reggie to repentance and purification in acknowledging Him. It blew my mind because it was the truth. While I was hellbent on exacting my plan of controlling Reggie's outcome or demise, thankfully, God used my attempt of revenge and included it in His plan. My marriage, the betrayal, my plan of revenge would all be used for His glory because He wasn't finished yet.

CHAPTER FIFTEEN

Never Letting Go of His Hand

The wise counsel God gives when I'm awake is confirmed by my sleeping heart. Day and night I'll stick with God ; I've got a good thing going and I'm not letting go. ~ Psalms 16:7-8 (MSG)

A few months after God intervened and blocked my plan of revenge, I settled into the fact my previous seasons of turmoil were taking a turn toward acceptance and peace. I continued to pray for my ex-husband. But, this time, I prayed for an apology from him. I relentlessly asked God to soften my ex's heart and move him to apologize for all the wrong I experience at his hands during our marriage. Although my marriage failed, and feelings of hurt and embarrassment lingered, I did my best to shift my focus towards the healing that I desperately needed.

With my heart and mind focused on myself, I took solace in my plan to work the businesses and move my life forward. The end of 2019 was vastly approaching, and I was days away from moving into an apartment when I received a call from the leasing manager five days before my move. She told me they had to deny my approval to move because of my dog's breed. I was completely thrown for a loop because of all the preparations I'd made. I secured a storage unit small enough to fit some things I didn't need but now I had to switch plans and get a bigger space, not to mention find another place to live. But before I became unnerved, I thought, "God, what are you up to now?" You see, over the past few months, I'd learn to look for God's hand in everything. Even the smallest of details could be Him speaking or directing me toward His will. So, I shrugged it off and trusted that He would provide as He had been doing the last year and a half for me.

The Big Shut Down

It was January 2020, and because I didn't move into the apartment, the decision was made to move in with my kids temporarily until I found another place. Let me stick a pin right here. When "I" (talking about me) look at all the bull I went through and everything I lost, it was a hard blow to my ego. Truthfully, some days, I felt as if I were in the twilight zone or a bad nightmare and couldn't wake up. On the other hand, to know more about God as I watched Him provide for me was equally mind-blowing. The moment He began revealing himself to me and showing me how He would carry me, my trust in Him deepened, and I just didn't worry about how He was going to do it. I was more anticipatory with when He would restore it all back to me. But before He would, I'd have to endure more attacks. Only this time, it was closer than I would have ever thought.

Okay, back to living with the kids. It hadn't been three weeks since moving in with them, and the enemy started to attack my relationship with them. I mean, enough was enough. I was sick and tired of being sick and tired of his attacks. I've heard it said before the only reason the enemy comes after you is because he considers you a threat. I was convinced that whatever God worked together for me would cause the enemy to loosen his grips on anything connected to me. I recognized his scheme to destroy yet another relationship connected to me right away. Just as I was close to getting up on my feet, mind and heart-healing, here he comes, raising his ugly head to try to threaten me again. Oh, but ya' girl was ready to stand in this fight. I wasn't playing defense this time. No, I was on offense because I was coming for him with everything God gave me.

The attack on my relationship with my children hurt me deeply because we had always been close when they were growing up. I mean nothing could separate us. But now, they were grown and had their ways of handling things, but yet relied upon momma from time to time. The strain on the relationship was too much too bare as fingers of blame pointed at each other as the silence became louder. I came out of one battle and went straight into another one over the course of eighteen months and quite honestly, I didn't know if I had the strength to go through another attack. So, because we weren't talking as a family, I had to talk to someone. And that someone was God.

My fight against the enemy began with God every Tuesday morning. I'd leave early in the morning, drive to a nearby park to read and pray. I didn't want anything to interrupt my time with God, especially with all the heaviness and bad energy at the kids' house because of the clashing of personalities, not to mention I was on their turf now and momma didn't make the rules. Nevertheless, I recognized it was spiritual warfare, and, this time, I had a few choice words to put him on the run.

During a time of devotion, God showed me that every attack in my life was connected to my relationships, whether a friend, family member, or significant other. And he didn't come at me with something new. No, he used the same ol' tricks of destroying the relationships that meant the most to me. Once I realized his tactic, I knew he was coming after what God was about to bring forth in my life, and I used my time with God to get a better understanding and revelation of what God was moving me to.

My Tuesday's with God was of complete surrender. I held nothing back. My mind was stronger, and I professed His word and reminded myself of who I was in Christ as God continued to remind me to be still. But by now, I knew that meant for me to keep trusting in Him. However, as I drew closer to God, the enemy turned up the heat of attacks from continued mood swings of emotions, struggles with growing my business, and attacks on my family.

God Showed His Hand Again

In early March, after a couple months of turmoil and discord within the house with my children and being in the middle of a vicious pandemic, I began praying and asking God to prepare me to move. I didn't ask Him if I could move; I declared I was going to move.

I continued my quiet time with God, which allowed me to hear from Him as I read His word and prayed over my life and the attack I was still under. The more time I spent with Him, the more surrendered I became to His will. I was no longer interested in doing things my way. I wanted everything He had for me, and I held nothing back when it came to what I felt and desired. Being in His presence was all I wanted.

In late June, I was sitting upstairs in my bedroom, and I got an impression on my heart to go to the store and buy some moving boxes. Because the feeling was so strong, I didn't second guess it; I obeyed what I felt in my heart and headed to the store to purchase the bins. Upon arriving home, I thought it was strange that I would consider moving in the middle of COVID-19 and in the middle of summer, but I thought to myself, "*God I'm ready for whatever you're take me*. There were no more thoughts about when or how because I knew God would show his hand again.

In the meantime, multiple efforts were made between me and my son to talk things out, and to get back to being in a better place, but nothing worked. We continued to butt heads and after all I had just gone through, I didn't have the strength to declare my "mom status" and demand the respect I felt I was due any more than I already had done. Moreover, it was more about being heard than right, so I didn't just wave the white flag, I put it down. I had no more fight left and didn't want to cause more damage than what had already been done. As angry as I was, I knew I had to let God work our yet another battle for me.

Go To Work God

In early August of 2020, during a conversation with a friend, she mentioned she struggled to hear from God. Our conversation was intense as I shared my struggles of hearing God and how He was teaching me to hear from Him. I had an opportunity to share all that God was doing with me with her and I held nothing back. As I shared with her my experience with listening for God's voice, she said I spoke about concerns she'd prayed about and she then realized that He did hear her and answered her concerns through our conversation. Our time on the phone was evident that God was in the middle of what she and I were going through. We couldn't do anything but celebrate the fact that God was in the midst of our conversation. Afterwards, we joined together in prayer, and as we ended the conversation, I said, "Go to work, God. Go to work!" I knew that God heard "that" prayer. And as it turned out, that day He indeed heard us.

Returning home, I felt lighter as I sat on the bed thinking about our prayer together. Roughly an hour later, I received a text from an unknown contact. It said, "I've been thinking about you and finally built up the courage to reach out to see how you're doing."

I responded, "It's good you thought of me, but who is this?" There was no response. Then it hit me. It was my ex-husband. I texted, "Is this, Reggie?" And before I knew it, my phone rang, and it was Reggie.

I answered and he immediately explained how he couldn't rest because I'd been on his mind. I was dumbfounded and wondered what God was up to now. I knew for certain God was behind his calling because I asked God to "go to work". Little did I know that He would work so fast and change my life.

The conversation started off with Reggie apologizing for how he handled our marriage, but more importantly, for accusing me of not believing in his business vision. He told me the reason he separated himself from me was to build his business how he wanted it, and he wasn't going to let anyone stop him, not even me. The moment arrived, after eighteen months; I finally got an apology from my ex-husband. I thought to myself, "*Thank you, Lord*".

The conversation continued and was mainly "catching up" talk. I was still amazed that Reggie called but even more anxious at what God was working together for my good. After a few minutes, Reggie asked if I believed prayer works. I told him yes and that I hadn't stopped praying for him since the day he left. He continued with his apologies, and as he did, every time he would say something I asked God for, I'd say, Thank You Lord. It was a slight whisper under my breath of thankfulness to God. After so many of my thanks, Reggie asked why I said it, and I told him God answered my prayers for an apology from him and each time I heard one I had to thank Him. He simply responded, "Humph, okay."

Reggie shared all that he was able to accomplish, the business success, the lavish lifestyle he had, and the multiple properties he'd acquired along with the house he bought for his parents. I remember him telling me years ago that all he wanted to do was take care of his parents and buy them a house. At least he was able to stay true to one promise he made. And yes, there was a bit of jealousy in me as I heard him brag about all of it. I told him how proud I was for him because that's all I ever wanted was for him to be successful. He went on to tell me how blessed he was and mentioned he had Jeremiah 29:11 etched on his foyer's wall. As he was speaking, I interrupted him and quoted the scripture. He appeared surprise and said, "Oh, you know about that huh?" I said, "Oh, of course, I know it." Only he had no clue how well I knew that scripture.

Reggie brought me up to date with his life and asked how I'd been. I told him everything was fine. I dare not tell him about the business being at a standstill. But my response wasn't good enough. "No, Rhlonda. Tell me how you're doing. I want to know how you're doing and where you're living." It was awkward because I felt he tried to read me as if I were the same person and he knew me so well. But I didn't go any further with it and answered him. Then he asked how he could help. To hear him ask me the question caught me by surprise. He had never offered to help me.

Like a deer in headlights, I couldn't do anything but pray and ask God for discernment, insight, help, direction and guidance. I needed all His help in that moment because I was completely caught off guard. For Reggie to ask me anything that looked remotely like concern was totally knew for me, so I knew God has to be in this conversation. Reggie asked again, "What do you need from me?" Everything in me wanted to scream as I thought, "*You fork-tongue fool, I want all of it! Every bit of what you took when you left. You do know you stole from me, tried to kill and destroy me, right?*" But I held back. I told him I didn't need anything from him, but I wanted to know why he asked after all the time that passed. He said he'd been thinking about it and after speaking with his mom, she told him to do what was on his heart. So, I blurted out, "I want my house back." To my surprise, he said, "Alright, cool. Do you have Cash App?" When I said yes, he told me to request $5,000 from him. I asked him why he'd give me $5,000. Surely this wasn't the man I knew before, and I damn sure wasn't going to get caught up in his schemes again. I didn't trust anything he said. He could tell I wasn't hearing what he said, so he insisted, "Just do it. I've been truly blessed, and I want to give back to the people who helped me get to where I am, and you're at the top of the list. I told you once before when I lock in on something I don't stop. Now I can do what I said I wanted to do for you." So, he gave me his information and confirmed the request. With my guards up, I thanked him for offering to help.

I knew God was up to something, but I never imagined that my help would come from the hand of the person who caused so much strife for me. Reggie, helping me? Huh, who would have thought such a thing could happen?

Reggie told me to find a place to live so that I could get back to doing everything I was supposed to do. He said, "I am going to pay your rent for a whole year." I thought it was a joke and asked if he were serious. He told me it was the least he could do.

The conversation eased up and as we continued talking about finding a place to live, I told him I had a vision board for my future house and texted him a picture. He said, "Wow, you're not going to believe this." He asked when I created the board and if I still had it. I told him yes. He gave me an address and told me to search the internet to pull it up. Upon seeing the house, I said, "Wow, this is nice."

He said, "This is my house that I paid cash for." I was stunned. He told me how crazy it was that everything on my vision board was what he had in his house. The rooms, layout, and the color scheme were identical to my board. Now, I had no idea where he lived before that day and I created the board months prior to his call. Was this a mere coincidence or something else? Still amazed at the similarities, I asked if he were serious.

He responded, "Yes, everything on your board is in my house. After a moment of silence, he said, "What if this is your house?"

I said, "Well, it's not because I don't live there."

"Well, what if you will in the future" he asked.

His comments were odd, but I went along and told him I didn't know anything about that because my house was on my board.

"Rhlonda, you need to know that your life is going to change very quickly," Reggie said. It will be very different within the next six months; trust me." He went on to say that he was a grown man now and repeated it with a proud tone in his voice. Reggie said, "I've always told you that you were going to get everything you wanted." I interrupted him and said, "Yeah, but you also made a vow to me when we married and you didn't keep that. "That's true, he responded, but I'm here now". I chuckled, "I don't know what to say about all that, but if you say so, okay."

Reggie said, "Trust it. Trust that you'll have everything you've said you've always wanted because *me* and God are going to restore you and make you whole again." "And just how are you going to do that", I asked. Reggie said to let him worry about that and just trust him. I couldn't help but laugh inside because of how he placed himself before God. Furthermore, that was a tall order to fill. Him giving me everything I ever wanted? Naw, that didn't sit well, but I said nothing. He asked if I was concerned about what people would say or what my family might think, but I didn't know where he was going with the questions so I told him I had learned to not focus on what anyone thinks because this was my life. He just said, "humph, okay, okay."

After we hung up, I thanked God for softening my ex-husband's heart to apologize. I was in awe of what God was doing. He was going to work, just as I asked. His hand was there from the beginning, and He was doing it in His timing and not mine. Plus, it was no coincidence that Reggie gave me $5,000 because that was certainly connected to me purchasing the storage bins two weeks prior. I had no idea God was working that into His plan. But I tell you, I wasted no time finding a rental house. I got approved and moved mid-August.

Old Habits Die Hard

Two weeks after moving, it was my birthday. I was headed home and wanted to give my ex-husband the details he requested after moving into the new house. I texted him several times but he didn't respond, which went on for a few days. Quite naturally, those old familiar emotions started resurfacing, me feeling Reggie was trying to pull the wool over my eyes. And like a dummy, I almost fell for it. But, I didn't because

I silently prayed for God to keep my focus on Him and not get ahead of what He was doing in this situation during our initial conversation.

During my time in St. Louis, the cycle of me texting and him not responding continued. I return home to Dallas, and after four days, still no word from Reggie. When I finally reached him, I could tell that something was wrong and discovered his mom fell ill and was in the hospital. Although I wanted to ask him about his offer, I decided not to mention it and told him we'd catch up later; but later turned into weeks.

While I waited for Reggie to call me back, I received a phone call from a gentleman who said he was from the company that held his contract. He asked if I would be willing to speak with one of their investigators in Memphis because he had more information to share with me via phone in a couple of days. I told him sure. I hung up the phone and thought to myself, *"Now they're investigating him after all this time?"*

No sooner than the thought left my mind, the phone rang, and it was the investigator from Memphis. He introduced himself and provided the preliminary statements that the investigation wasn't about me but the previously reported information. After he brought me up to speed on what had taken place and the amount of fraud that transpired, I decided to listen to the questions and the information that he had and play it easy. I answered the questions as vaguely as possible until I could figure out what was going on. In other words, I needed to pray to God about this thing.

He questioned me about my Reggie's finances when we were married, details of the contract, driver's names, signed invoices, and any business roles I had. I told him what I knew about the contract and the daily amount for the driver's pay, which was only what Reggie "shared" with me. After answering his questions, he said that he would follow up if he thought of additional questions.

After speaking with the investigator, I continued trying to contact Reggie but had no luck in reaching him. My last attempt was made in early October from my business line, knowing he wouldn't recognize the number. I texted and told him I was on my way to his house to talk. He immediately replied and said, "No, who is this?" After telling him it was me; he called me back right away. Before jumping into the discussion, I had with the investigator, I asked him how things was going since he hadn't responded to any calls or texts. Quite honestly, I was contemplated sharing what I knew with him, so I needed to set the tone of the conversation first. He explained his driver was involved in an accident had a lawsuit against him, and the driver was suing for $650,000. Of course, he exaggerated the story, but I knew better. So, I let him continue to see if he would be truthful about what was shared with me. He told me he needed to amend his offer to pay my rent. Instead of paying my rent for one year, he could only give me another $5k, and he would let me know soon when he would give the money to me. I left well-enough alone and decided not to mention the investigator. I went along with what Reggie said and we hung up the phone.

As I replayed the conversation, I knew that he was telling me a bold-faced lie. He hadn't changed. I thought back to our conversation earlier, and the smoke from my nostrils and ears started to roll. He bragged about not driving his truck anymore since he had fifteen drivers and made $30,000 per week since he'd been gone. Yes, I know he offered me to "make me whole again," but I'm not blind, crippled, or crazy. I got upset, realizing he hadn't changed. He was more interested in keeping up appearances than show his crooked hand.

Desperate to figure out the real meaning behind Reggie contacting me, I removed myself from the chaos of it all so God could show me the truth. And, after a while, it began making sense. My businesses were fading fast. God blocked the attempts and paused the investment I put into the brokerage/ parking lot. It became clear that what I spent time and energy doing wasn't in His plan for me. He allowed me to get only so far with that project and then it came to a complete standstill. Nothing panned out. Even the contractors and the banker couldn't understand it. He was protecting me from making a huge mistake that would take me years to come up from under. God had my full attention though when He brought Reggie back into the picture to reroute my business plans. Come to think of it, the truck parking lot was another attempt at forcing something to work from my marriage. And, it too failed.

But get this; God hadn't forgotten about me and heard my prayers. He used the person who caused me major loss to move me in the direction of where He needed me, and that was Reggie. He did it through the hands of my ex-husband, but God was in charge all along because I was almost to the point of believing what my ex-husband told me. God showed His hand again, but this time, He revealed there would be consequences to my ex-husband's actions. I guess if I was ever to see justice from God in my life, it would be with Reggie. There was no need for me to be impatient for God to act, I needed to keep moving steadily in His ways and He would exalt me at the right time.

After I hung up with my ex-husband, I felt a disdain for him like no other. I was so angry that he thought he could manipulate and lie to me once again. I sent him a text and told him that we could talk when he quit lying and hiding the truth. When he got the text, he called back, saying he was confused. He stuck his chest out about how he put up the money for me to move. Everything was he did this, that, and the other. Well, the last "I" he said sent me reeling on his ass. I completely lost it. I called him a fraud, a con artist, and a liar. And since I was on a roll, I told him he hadn't changed because everything was still about him. I told him he should have never put God in his lie about making me whole because he would soon see God's hand.

Then something happened. There was a shift in my attitude toward Reggie. I told him that he had some dark days ahead of him, but I would be there for him. I would be there because I knew what it felt like to lose everything. Especially when it's ripped away, and you have no one while you're in a place of isolation. I assured Reggie the only way I could do that is because God allowed me to go through it first and strengthen me to be there for the next person and from my point of view it was him.

I told him I knew everything about the fraud, investigation, and potential charges against him. Everything in me wanted to ask why he would do such a thing, but I couldn't stomach another lie from Reggie. After all was said and done, in a very controlled manner he said, "Well, I guess that's all that needs to be said then." I told him, "You're exactly right, but know I will be there for you." We hung up.

Letting Go of "his" Hand

Over the next few weeks, the investigator contacted me questioning Reggie's drivers. The information they had on him was piling up until I just couldn't stomach it much longer. I was completely stunned how he manipulated the names of the drivers; using some first names, some last names and a mixture of some. I guess it's true when they say the golf course is where a lot of "business" deals are closed. But even more than that, I was sickened by one name in particular the investigator mentioned. But I guess if he could betray me, he most certainly could betray one of his own. Hanging up from speaking with the investigator, I cried so hard and had thoughts of calling Reggie, but didn't. It was too much to bear and it wasn't my cross to carry any longer. I cried for days thinking of how low Reggie would go for money that I knew I had to release him completely.

During my devotional time with God a few weeks later, I prayed for my ex-husband. It was difficult to shake the feeling of what he did and thought he would never get caught. I felt sorry for him because of the brevity of his actions. I told God that when or if Reggie had to face his actions and pay for all the wrong he'd done, I wanted to be there for him. God, in all His humor, immediately moved on me to pray for him immediately. As I prayed for Reggie, I understood God loved him too. I sat in the presence of God's love and felt it directly for Reggie. All I could do was cry for him but rejoice that God had him too because the chiseling God spoke to me about Reggie would no doubt, soon begin. I can admit, I was still furious, but I understood God's grace entirely, and who was I not to extend it to my ex-husband. Little did I know the last interaction with Reggie, was met with open arms to release him and all that we had experienced together as well as apart.

I knew it was God who orchestrated the contact between Reggie and me. Thirteen months passed since our divorce, and God finally revealed why He'd been silent. I now understand that I underwent spiritual surgery sitting in isolation with God while He prepared to me to see justice His way. He started the process of restoration, but it would be better than I could ever imagine. Better, because this was about my healing and not about Reggie. God was restoring my heart and showed me the hidden blessings of protection, provision, and His sustaining power I couldn't see before. No amount of money or material things could ever take the place of wholeness.

October 2020, the investigator contacted me to advise the case was going to be presented to the defrauded companies to determine the outcome of the case. To this day, I don't know what ever became of Reggie's case, but I still call him every now and then just to check on him. I still sit at the feet of God and continued to let Him heal my heart. I've committed myself to Him and it's all because I am trust that everything I need is at the hand of Him.

CHAPTER SIXTEEN

His Teaching Hand

Teach me more about you, how you work and how you move, so that I can walk onward in your truth until everything within me brings honor to your name. ~Psalms 86:11 (TPT).

Let me ask you a question? Did you notice how jacked up my emotions were throughout my experience? You know, the back and forth, repetition of wanting my heart's desire, and continually crying out to God. Did you notice that? Well, I did that purposefully to show even with our best intentions and turning to God, we still struggle. I struggle to believe what I pray for will come to pass sometimes. I struggle with doubts and trusting God at the same time. I struggle with emotions taking over. So, yes, the struggle is real. And I know that is okay because the heart is real, and when it's torn because of the considerable amount of love we invest, it takes time to realign. So, instead of beating myself up for my array of feelings, I started to trust it's in that place that God will do His best work in me, and you too.

Through the healing process from Reggie's betrayal, God

blessed me with a new outlook on life. Yes, it's true that I wanted to recoup all that the material possessions I'd lost at the hands of my ex-husband, But I truly believe I gained more at the hand of God. My hope had been restored that things will be worked out in the end. Maybe not how we expect it but nonetheless, it somehow works out.

I personally understand what it means to be made in His image. His healing helped me come out of betrayal into being whole, refreshed, and undeniably grateful for His love toward me. Now, when I talk with God, I'm honest with Him about everything and I don't feel like I'm being punished when I tell Him about my mistakes. It's easy for me to share my true feelings with Him because of His never-ending love toward me.

I love the woman I am now and I'm learning how to love me more, flaws and all. I no longer blame myself for things that happened to me nor do I feel unworthy to receive everything good thing that He has for me. I pursue what I want and desire and I'm clinging to peace, happiness, love, and look forward to a life fully complete in God. Sure, it scares the crap out of me to wait patiently as I discover what God unfolds for me in the next chapter of life, but I have seen His hand and I'm sure He won't leave me disappointed.

Of course, I still find it challenging to let go of trying to control situations and trust God. But I'm much better at recognizing it and release it over to Him as I remind myself to "be still" and trust Him in all things. And get this, I hear Him telling me this all the time now.

There's no doubt that reading the word of God helped me to speak His promises over my life. He opened my heart to receive the truth of His word and closed my mouth from negative talk. How I handled trials before left me trapped by the lies of the enemy. But God pulled me closer to Him to discipline and build His character within me. And for that, I'm grateful.

1 Peter 5:10 (TPT) says, "And then, after your brief suffering, the God of all loving grace, who has called you to share in his eternal glory in Christ, will personally and powerfully restore you and make you stronger than ever. Yes, he will set you firmly in place and build you up."

Therefore, I've come to the conclusion that I will never let go of HIS HAND!

P.S.

I'm trading everything I'm not, for who I am. I'm going deeper into spiritual surgery and I'll see you on the other side of the bandages.

The Hidden Blessings

There were some very valuable lessons I learned, and I certainly would like to share them with you here. If you are moved to do so, please make sure you get the full companion guide and devotional, *Hidden B'Lessons At the Hands of Him*. Trust me they apply to every area of our lives. Allow Him to teach you under His loving hand.

Are you ready?

Lesson #1 – Are you being still long enough?

When we look for God's hand and can't find him, it' isn't because he's not there; it's because we've moved. Whether we moved from spending time with Him or "things" moved into the place of priority in our lives, it may seem as if He's no longer there. Often, we focus more on our situation or what we're going through than turning to or searching for Him, which may cause us to take action and leave God in the dust.

Have you ever heard the saying "you can't trust what you can't trace?" Well, it's different with God. He wants us to trust Him even when we can't trace Him. God Holy Word says, be still and know. Know what? Know that He is God (Psalms 46:10). He is the great "I am." He is ____. You fill in the blank and I know He can be that too, but you have to be still and let Him be what you are seeking.

Distractions, circumstances, and the issues that consume us make it difficult to see God work in our lives, let alone hear Him. But God's word tells us to move our hearts closer to Him, and He will come even closer (James 4:8-TPT). And the only way to do that is by leaning into Him or by being still.

Please don't get ahead of God and what He's doing. Don't take matters into your hands. God promises us that when we trust Him with our whole heart and release the way we think things should be, He will direct our paths. We will find his hand in the details and the circumstances of life every time. If you get quiet and be still long enough to seek God wholeheartedly, you will see he's moving and hear him too.

Now let's be clear, I'm not saying that's easy to do. However, what I am saying now is that it's necessary. Resisting being still with God will only make it more challenging to see God working in your life. Take it from me; God is not going to force himself on us. He's patient with us and will wait until we're obedient.

Let this rock your world; God doesn't think like us (thank goodness), and His ways are not ours (Isaiah 55:8). So, before we tell God how, when, and what we want him to do in our lives, we'd better pump the brakes. No matter how hard we try, we cannot manipulate God into our plans for our lives. Ha! I "soooo" tried him and failed miserably. But what we can do is stop, reflect, and ask God some critical questions; "God, where are you in this situation? What are you trying to show me as I seek you?" Then you will be in a position not only to see God's hand but also trust his hand.

Lesson #2-Timing is everything!

God's timing is perfect, not ours. We may think we're ready for something, and before you know it, we're all out in traffic, unprotected. When you find yourself in God's waiting room, be patient and persistent. Oh, okay. So, you don't want to wait anymore? You want to get past waiting and back to life, right? Well, I have some good news and some good news. Timing is everything. Think about it; we wait until the time is right to purchase a home or a car, make career changes, plan the perfect vacation, amongst other things. Do you get my drift? So, why is it the most challenging thing for us to do when waiting on God's timing? I mean, He is the Master of time, right?

Look at what His word says about time; "God made everything beautiful in itself, and in its time-but He's left us in the dark, so we can never know what God is up to (Ecclesiastes 3:11-Msg). He has made everything beautiful in its time. He has put eternity in their hearts, except that no one can find out the work that God does from beginning to end."

Did you catch that? God makes everything beautiful when--in its time. Not yours and certainly not mine. So, whatever "it" is that you're waiting for God to do, rest in the fact of knowing that when it arrives, it will not only be on time but beautiful.

Now, I don't know about you, but that ole' leaving us in the dark seems a little daunting. Why would God want to leave us in the dark? Allow me to help you out here. He leaves us in the dark because He knows all the incredible, beautiful, good, and perfect gifts He has in store for us. He also knows that we will get way ahead of ourselves if He just let us know everything, he's planning for us. God is faithful, and we're not because we fall short of his glory every time. He knows we would run off ahead and without him. So, he teaches us to walk with him and at His leading—Whew Chile', that's a word for somebody. Go right ahead and rest on that one for a minute. How wonderful it would be if we trust God to make everything for us beautiful and not just in time but on time.

Lesson #3-You might get picked!

Listen! Listen! Ain't nobody in their right mind saying "pick me" to go through what Job in the Bible went through. But did you notice that God picked Job? Now I'm not saying that God caused chaos, hurt, and devastation in Job's life, but I am saying God-Picked-Job. Let's be clear about that one. Go back and read the story.

God shows us through Job's experience that we may be faithless, but God will remain faithful (2 Timothy 2:13). I'm talking to those of you who've lost faith that God can do the impossible. Yep, your situation seems impossible. But, let me remind you, is there anything too hard for God? (Genesis 18:4, Jeremiah 32:27). No matter what it looks like and how fearful you are, know that when God is in it, or even when He offers you up, he will sustain and restore you. When God is in it, nothing, not one thing, will be lost.

I believe God wants to share with us two things from Job's story: our response and his restoration. First, how we respond to trials is significant to the outcome and our relationship with God. Consider, are you going to trust God, or are you going to blame him for everything and put him on trial? Well, I've done both. And if you would be honest, so have you. But, while I pointed my finger, I still praised him like Job, but I fell short. Job said nothing against God. I didn't do all the extras like praying when I thought my children "possibly sinned." No, that wasn't me. I was the chick that prayed most times when something happened, not before. Now, I'm much better, but Job had ya' girl beat by a long shot. My point is our response to heartbreak, and unfair situations are what God is most concerned about; he's interested in our response and how we react. Think about it; he may be testing you to see if you'll be faithful and praise him through your trials.

Secondly, God is a God who restores. It's not because we deserve it, but because that's who He is. Not only restore but avenge us (Proverbs 20:22). If we are willing to wait on God and his timing, he will not leave us without what's best. He restores fully. The Bible assures us that even when we are in over our heads with trials, God will get us going again and better than before (Psalms 71:20-21 TPT). So, that settles what He says. Now, believe it. Let me help you. Please don't respond like I did, shaking my fist at God, trying to manipulate him to go along with my terms of how he should handle things. Instead, respond like God knows what he's doing. Don't grumble. Instead, praise your way through. Take it from me; it lifts your spirits. And once your response is that of gratitude and thanksgiving, you'll see God begin to put your life back together and better than ever before.

Lesson #4 If you speak it, look for it.

Have you ever stopped to think that some of the things we experience is a direct result of the words we've spoken? Just think about that for a minute. Our heart's position determines what we think and, ultimately, what we say. And what we say will determine life or death in every situation we face. The more we focus on what could go wrong, they will. The more that things go wrong, we become depressed. I'll also add that when depression increases, our faith will decrease.

In my book, "At the Hands of Him", there is chapter titled "Hand of Darkness" where I certainly went through darkness all because the enemy spoke many lies to me, which I started believing. Eventually, I spoke them into my previous marriage.

Listen, I can't stand the devil. Did you hear me? I said I can't stand our enemy. But I can't blame him either because he did what he does best; lie. During that time in my life, he didn't act out of character, I did. He had a field day with my "idle" mind because every negative thought was birth months before my husband left. Seeds of doubt, frustration, and worry is what I planted in my head on early in my marriage, although for good reasons. However, the difference is I didn't tear them down, I let them grow. They grew until my mind was just like a forest filled with trees of hatred, resentment, doubts, anger, and bitterness, and so dense that everything about my marriage was dark. There was no way light could break through and the slippery slope begins. Negative thoughts lingering become dark. Next, you speak negativity and darkness into your life. And that's where the enemy wants us right before he comes in for the kill.

Whatever fills your heart will spill from your mouth. So, may I offer a piece of advice? Get control over your thoughts as quickly as possible if you want to survive difficult times.

Do everything in your power to fend off destructive thoughts. If you don't, you'll be stuck and with no peace of mind. We determine if the fruit we eat will be life-giving or death-ending (Proverbs 18:21), and I didn't want those negative seeds to control my mind, nor choke the life out of me. Do you? So again, I implore you; whatever you speak, look for it, because it's sure to happen (good or bad).

Lesson #5 Put it on the run!

Many of you may be familiar with the Bible scripture that says, "So then, surrender to God. Stand up to the devil and resist him and he will turn and run away from you", James 4:7 (TPT). I love this verse (especially the Message version). I want you to pay attention to the "call to action" in this scripture. There are three of them, and two belong to you and me.

1. Surrender to God – give everything to him. Whatever the situation is, release it to him (Us)
2. Stand up to the devil and resist him – I love this because it tells me that I can confront the enemy instead of him always coming after me and stand my ground of not giving in to him (whew Chile that's good) (Us)
3. He will run (with his tail between his legs)

Okay, those are my words, but you get the drift. He's gotta go. Bye-Bye, you little imp. The message Bible says to "yell a loud no to the devil and watch him scamper, say a quiet Yes to God, and He'll be there in no time. Do you see the difference here? When you wage war against the devil, you have to get loud and boisterous with him. You can't go into war whispering like a chump. No, you have to get "jiggy" with him and use all the authority God gave you. But with God, a quiet yes gets his attention, and He's right there.

Lesson #6 What you don't want can't stay.

The enemy is cunning and crafty. He will try to lead you to a place you do not want to go. Sometimes, when we face some of life's challenges, we often believe the lies he's trying to tell us. Once you believe the lies, he will do any and everything to keep you there as you rehearse the pain. The trick is to keep you focused on the lie. The thoughts and emotions, or even actions, may start small. The next thing you realize is that you're so far gone; he will have you believe there is no hope, and you may as well stay stuck. Well, that's a LIE from the father of lies (John 8:44). I need you to shout it loud with me, "he can't stay, and he can't win!"

God will help you stand up to the enemy and cancel his lies. Can you wait until you "feel" better? Nope. I implore you to search God's truth and hold it against every lie the enemy tries to tell you.

- Satan will suggest that we're unloved, but God says we are the apple of his eye.
- Satan may lead you to believe you're a nobody, but God says you are his prized possession.
- Satan will have us to think we are defeated, but God says we are victorious.
- Satan throws everything at us to make us afraid, but God says we have power, love, and a sound mind (thank you, God).
- Satan will try and convince us that we don't belong to Christ, but God says we are in right standing with him through Christ.

BAM!. Satan can't win! Everything the enemy tries to accuse me of (and you too), there's a counter-response in the Word of God that will put the enemy on MUTE. Shhh! Do you hear that? Ha, me either. No more lies from the enemy. Moreover, God promises that the enemy will not harm us no matter what we walk or pass through on our journey in life. So, I think it's worth saying again-Satan can't win!!!

Lesson #7 Nothing is always something.

I want to encourage you that when God's hand is on your life, He's either moving you towards or away from something. You may not always recognize it at the moment. And, you don't always know what He's doing. But trust me, He's doing something. A friend always says to her clients to "trust the process." My Goodness, that is a word for somebody. Did you know that nothing is something to God? He can work a "nothing" into your situation and cause it to produce something you would have never imagined. Now, I don't know about you, but I'll take God's nothing over anybody's something any day of the week. You wanna know why? Because somebody's something just might fall short of my need. Their something is "iffy," so you risk taking a chance with just any ole' somebody. But God's nothing (humph), that's always for your good, and it is entirely what the situation needs. Best believe it. So, remember, when anybody asks for your order, tell them you want a good helping of God's nothing. Please sit back and wait on the preparation. Satisfaction guaranteed.

Lesson #8 There will be nothing wasted.

Whether good, bad, or indifferent, every experience in life is necessary to make it on the journey that leads us towards God's plan for our lives. Every experience is needed. Each one plays a significant part in God's plan for our lives. That's why the Bible encourages us not to give up doing good things, for there will be a reward. So, when we find ourselves in situations where we have experienced hurt, pain, trials, and struggles, all of those things are resources needed to build us along the journey. What God has for our lives requires some of these to be used in His plan. There will be no waste as every detail will be used.

If we pay close enough attention, we will begin to see God's plan for our lives in the patterns of our experience. There is a pattern attached to God's plan for your life, and he will use them to birth His plan that he has uniquely designed for you.

Even in our mess, let's be clear; He can take everything that we do and use it to turn in our favor. Just because we're looking for God to do what we've prayed a certain way, and He does it another, doesn't mean that God is not working on our behalf. On the contrary, He's considering everything—all of our decisions, all of our prayers, yes, everything God considers. Trust me; He's taking it all into consideration. All you have to do is look back over your life, look for any patterns that bring you joy, cause your heart pain, or urge you to help solve a problem. Those are desires or longings that God has placed inside of you. They are part of His plan for you, which in turn, will bring him glory as you live out His calling for your life. The best part of it all is He's working on bringing together this incredible masterpiece for our lives to bring him glory.

Lesson #9 Get off that throne!

Do you ever feel like you don't have control in some areas of your life? Well, let me tell you a "sumpting" I learned during a dark season in my life; I sat on the throne of pride. My image was at stake because of everything I had before I lost it, and there was no way I was going down without a fight. The ugly truth about it was I'd succumb to arrogance when I thought I could take over what I entrusted God to handle. God exposed what was hidden deep in my heart, control issues. My actions were justified excuses, which caused me to become stagnant in reasoning. I was defiant to the knowledge of God and what he intended to do in my life.

I'm confident that we feel out of control because we don't allow the pain from circumstances to produce purpose in us. We go against the grain of God's intentions; we grumble and complain (at least I did) because every ounce of the pain is real. But take it from me, we can't allow the pain to push us to be disgruntled and bitter at the person that caused the offense or God. Instead, we should place our cares in the lap of God and wait as He massages them. The longer you sit with God, the more he will loosen you up, and before you know it, you're walking, flexing, and moving at a pace you weren't before. But that's if you don't fight against it.

I had to learn a sobering lesson about control and forcing the outcome to be how I thought it should be for me. I would stay in that situation, and God would have me fight, toss and turn, tumble, and stay down in those painful moments. That's when I realized I had to do it his way because it would continue to cause me much angst, bitterness, and unrest if I didn't. When I released control, He started massaging the pain and turning it into moments of reflection, forgiveness, and worship. Then, I went back to being my true self and the person He created me to be. Friend, He will do the same thing for you if you give it all to him. Just remember, keeping our hands on the reigns of our problems will prolong us seeing God be the "I AM" in our life. So, let's all agree that we will give God the lead in our lives so He can be and do all that He desires for us.

Lesson # 10 For the Love of it.

I've said many times over my life that love is an action word. I believed it was a tingly feeling towards another person or an intense feeling of deep affection. Ha! Boy, did I have this one wrong (somewhat anyway)? Later in life, God showed me that love was not what I thought it was. Love is about giving and not so much a feeling.

But where does it start, and where should it go? Well, let's see. Think about this for a minute, if I love someone no matter what they do, say, deserve, or not, I will always demonstrate love, right? Of course. But how is that possible? It's possible because the Holy Spirit's indwelling allows me to give love and keep on giving it when I understand the kind of love He has towards me. Because God's spirit of love resides in me, he equips me with the same kind of love I should give to others. It wasn't us that loved first; it was God.

When you realize how much God loves you – with an extravagant, irresistible, unconditional love – then His love will change your entire focus on how you care for others. On the other hand, if we don't receive God's love for us, we'll have a hard time loving other people. I'm sure you will agree with me that it's pretty hard to love some folks we know. I'm talking about loving the unlovely, loving the difficult, loving the irritable, loving people who are annoying or demanding. That doesn't negate God's commanded to love our neighbors the same way we love ourselves. Self comes after loving God and then our neighbor.

But here's the dilemma. If we don't love ourselves, we will undoubtedly find it difficult to show love to someone else. Yep. We can do everything for them and still not have love in our hearts. Just remember, God is more concerned with why you do something for someone than what you do. It's entirely possible to do the right thing but with the wrong attitude or motive. Let your motive have its center in love.

Lesson #11 It fits like a puzzle piece.

Nothing in your life is accidental or coincidental. The pleasures and pains, the opportunities and obstacles, God can use it all. There is nothing God cannot use for good in your life if only you would hand it over to him. Every detail of your life experiences fit together like pieces of a puzzle. Consider those times we are joyful, and things are going well; there are details from each interwoven with the times that are not so pleasant but often challenging. There's something far more important than our pain, and that should be the lessons we learn from them.

God knows the reasons, the causes, and the things that many times push us to our breaking point. He knows, and he cares. Of course, we can ask God to remove difficult situations and life challenges from our lives. Chances are he probably won't because we live through it to discover later that those lessons were the very things God used to shape and build His character within us.

Think about puzzle pieces for a moment. They have different shapes, sizes, curved, straight, and pointed edges. Much like our life, we experience big and small challenges. We go straight through a challenge, but we often have twists and turns as we go through difficult times. And let's not forget about those that poke at our heart with sharp edges of disappointments and frustrations. Just like those puzzle pieces, each one fits into the big picture that God is designing for our lives. When we try to control things in our strength by worrying, in essence, what we're doing is taking responsibility for something God never intended for us to carry, much like forcing a piece of the puzzle into a space that doesn't fit. In the end, the good thing is that God knows how the picture of his plan will look like in the end. We have to trust him with the pieces of our life.

Lesson #12 Can you hear me now?

Have you ever questioned if God hears you? Let me assure you he hears every word you speak. The fact is that sometimes we're so busy or distracted with so much clutter around us that we believe that He's not listening or speaking to us. But that's not the case. God speaks to us in different ways that He fashions for each of us. His voice is designed for you because he knows that you will become familiar with that specific voice if only, we take the time to tune in to it.

As I went through a difficult separation and divorce, there were times that God reminded me that He was listening. There were times I'd have conversations with him, but it felt as if I was talking to my best friend, Bev. Now, I know that may sound strange to you, but I could hear her voice encouraging me. Later God revealed to told me it was actually him talking to me. I'm convinced he did that because he knew that I was familiar with my friends' voice and trusted her. He wanted to be just as close to me as I was to her. Whenever I need to hear from God, I'd get somewhere quiet, and he would speak in my voice (inner spirit), or I heard him within a conversation between my best friend and me, although she was nowhere around.

God will use whatever means it takes to communicate with

us. If you allow yourself to let him teach you his voice, you can talk with God every day. He will lead you, and you will see his hand leading you in whatever you're going through. The key is being willing to listen.

Listen and learn the voice of God the way that He wants to speak to you. He will always speak to you through His Word. When you hear that small intimate voice of God during those moments, you're thinking deeply about something or having a conversation in your heart; allow the Holy Spirit into the conversation. You will hear him speak back to you.

Lesson #13 God is still good in the bad times.

Have you ever blamed God when bad things happen to you? I know I have. But I want to be clear that God doesn't allow anything "bad" to happen to us. Just think about what he says in Jeremiah 29:11. So, let me say that again. God does not orchestrate bad things to come against us. Moreover, there isn't one descriptive thing about God in his Word relative to hurting his children or that He's bad.

So, the first thing that we need to do is stop asking, "why did God do this to me?". He didn't. He's not the blame for what someone else did to you. But He takes what happens and says, "Ah, this is a good time for me to put my child's character on display and mold it into the character of my beloved son, Jesus Christ."

God will take that horrible thing and use it to help you. Even while He's using the bad experience, it may hurt. There may even be disappointments and disruptions. Yep, even some isolation, along with a host of other things happening. But trust that He's going to use it and turn it around into something useful. Why? Because everything is working together, even the bad stuff. The Bible says all things work together for good (not bad); to those who love him and called according to His purpose (Romans 8:28). And if you know that you are in Christ, then you already know that His purpose for you is not to harm you but to prosper you and to give you hope and a future (Jeremiah 29:11).

So that settles it; he's still good. Everything about God is good. Oh, taste and see that the Lord, He is good (Psalms 34:8). He uses our bad experiences to teach, prune, and grow us. And they will turn out good. Let's be careful not to blame God, as I did, for letting my husband leave and take everything I worked hard for years. My ex-husband chose to leave, not God. And, every choice has a result, and every decision has a consequence, good or bad. Trust God to turn them around. Remember, we have to move forward and know that whatever is happening, God is using it altogether, and it's working for us, not against us.

Lesson #14 Part-ownership?

There are some areas in life where we decide we need to move from partnership to ownership. We move from renting to owning a house or car. We may have worked for a company for a while and decide it's time to become a business owner. Even in relationships, we move from girlfriend/boyfriend to husband/wife status where we feel we "own" them now because they are solely ours. In other words, what I'm trying to say is we catch what I like to call the "spirit of take-over." Have you been there too?

Well, that's not how it should be in our relationship with God. We actually should be pursuing the opposite for our lives, ownership to a partnership. God wants us to partner with him, and we should be excited about that. But no, when we think we have all the answers and how we want to do things, we think we are leveling up, taking over, and doing it the best way for everybody's good. But in actuality, we're about to mess some stuff up. We will especially miss the "level" that God wants to take us to. Then guess what happens? We find ourselves in a situation smothered in arrogance and pride, all because we want the boss's seat. When you stop to think about it, he tells us he owns everything anyway, so why would we ever think we can move God out of his place at the head of our lives? It would be foolish to think that the price God paid for you through his son Jesus Christ wasn't enough for him to know how to partner with you. But here's the kicker about God and his graciousness, he will let you think you've taken ownership only for so long. When life happens, and you come to your senses, you will be running back to the father to take your rightful place. Just ask the prodigal son. So, let's be in partnership with God to experience all that he has for us, moving us from glory to glory. Don't get ahead and operate outside of the Glory of God.

Lesson #15 God isolates to insulate.

In 2020 COVID-19 caused most of us, if not all, isolation from family, friends, and co-workers. Because of the deadly infection, we had to wear masks, practice social distancing, wash our hands often, and, depending on the circumstances, quarantine ourselves. The rapid spread of the virus caused the entire world to shut down instantly, resulting in the government issuing "stay at home" orders for several months. And as we know, after an extended period of being cooped up and feelings of isolation, it took a toll on a lot of folks.

Well, before there was such a virus, I went through my own isolation experience at the hand of God. God covered my mouth to protect myself and others because I spoke negatively about my divorce. He had me in isolation or, may I say, "socially distant" me from others so I could sit alone to discover who I was in him and learn all about who He was to me. As he worked in me, I quarantined so I wouldn't infect others around me. God took the time to heal me, cleanse me, and sanitize me from the germs the enemy tried to infect me. This process continued for months, just like COVID-19 did for the entire world.

So, let me ask, who really wants to be isolated? Not too many of us, right? But, when God takes time to isolate us, it's because He wants us to become more intimate with him, pulling us away from all the distractions to purge us from everything that moves us further away from him. That's the place where we're all alone with him.

Isolation can be useful to remove us from hurtful experiences while God is repairing the insulation around us that's worn off. You know, the protective traits we used to carry with us like kindness, forgiveness, or patience. They deplete. We're an easier target for the arrows the enemy shoots at us. Harsh words penetrate our hearts, and we react how we didn't before. So, what does God Do? He has to set us apart to insulate and saturate us in His Word to strengthen us again.

In isolation, he's protecting, pruning, and proving us to be His children. We shouldn't view isolation as a bad thing. Now, it might feel like punishment in the IR (isolation room). But we should listen to the voice of God and be attentive to what He's teaching us. When God strips things away, remove idols in our lives, or even people with malicious motives, that's him protecting us. His loving motive is to strengthen, rebuild, and reshape us.

Can the isolation room be a blessing? Of course, because you're spending time with God, and He can show you who you are and how valuable you are to him. He is building godly characteristics in you. So, by the time you walk out of that horrible situation and out of isolation, you will be insulated with the power of God actively working within you. You'll have His protection around you, your mind will be healthier, your body will be fit, and your heart will have protection from now on better than the previous experience.

When God moved me into a place of isolation, I believe God was saying to me, "I don't want you to put anything above me. I want you to get to know me so intimately that whatever comes your way, it's going to bounce off of you because I have insulated you in my love, strength, power, and in my image. And until you get to know me on that level, everything that happens to you will trigger you, frustrate you, push you over the limit, and you're going to react in a way that is not of me. So I'm leading you to the isolation room to get reacquainted where I can insulate you. And when I finish, you'll see yourself in a whole new way and respond to life my way."

So, go with God into the isolation room so he can insulate you. It's the best spa experience you will ever have, and you'll leave feeling refreshed, renewed, and empowered.

Wow! We made it through my journey. Thank you so much for allowing me to share my story with you. But we're not done just yet. Now I get to talk directly to you, my friend. Yes, you. You see, you've got a chance to hear my story, but you have a story too. Now it's my turn to encourage and remind you that you're not alone. And I want to hear all about it. Trust me, I'm not trying to be nosey but to share what reality is like for some if not most of us. Unlike reality TV we've seen over the years, I want to hear from the regular ole' Mary, Paula, and Lisa's of the world. Oh, and you – you can add your name here as well. I want to hear from you. We can encourage one another as we all heal from betrayal and move into the handy little blessings God has for us.

So how do we stay connected?

Sign up to stay tuned to upcoming podcast, devotionals, and guests who want to share their stories. Together, we're better when we share our testimonies.

Visit atthehandsofhim.com and let's stay connected!

See you soon!

Can You Help?

Thank You for Reading My Book!

I really appreciate all of your feedback, and I love hearing what you have to say.

I need your input to make the next version of this book and my future books better.

Please leave me an honest review on Amazon letting me know what you thought of the book.

Thanks so much!

Rhlonda Washington

ABOUT THE AUTHOR

Rhlonda Washington, born and raised in St. Louis, Missouri, is a mother of two adult sons, an entrepreneur, and has been a Human Resources professional for over 18 years and currently resides in Dallas, Texas. For more than 30 years, Rhlonda has kept pen and paper nearby as she journals her life experiences, creating prayers and other resources from the Word of God to keep her faith grounded in God. Rhlonda is passionate about helping people who have experienced heartbreak in relationships by offering words of encouragement. Rhlonda prefers to "keep it real" as she shares her experiences and her ability to bounce back through her relationship with God. "At the Hands of Him" is her first book.

You can stay connected with Rhlonda at www.atthehandsofhim.com to learn more about her upcoming podcast and other inspirational resources.

Devotional Guide Also Available

AtTheHandsOfHim.com/Available-books

Made in the USA
Las Vegas, NV
12 April 2021